EMBRACING CHATGPT FOR BUSINESS SUCCESS

SIMPLIFIED DIGITAL SOLUTIONS TO ENHANCE
EFFICIENCY, GAIN ADVANTAGE, AND OPTIMIZE COST
FOR ENTREPRENEURS SKEPTICAL ABOUT EMERGING
AI TECHNOLOGIES

DBR PUBLISHING

This book is dedicated to the entrepreneur who introduced Dr. Bryan Raya to ChatGPT, his dear friend and colleague, Adam Robison. A special thanks to all the entrepreneurs and small business owners who shared insights for this book.

"A.I. will not take over the world.
The people that harness the power of A.I. will."
-Adam Robison,
Northwest Arkansas Business Radio X

CONTENTS

FOREWORD

In "Embracing ChatGPT for Business Success" Dr. Bryan Raya, the driving force behind DBR Publishing, DBR Bookkeeping, and the Doing Business Right podcast, shares his unwavering commitment to helping small business owners and entrepreneurs thrive in today's dynamic landscape. Following the success of his first book, "The Essential Small Business Guide to Financial Management," Dr. Raya continues his mission to empower small business owners with the knowledge and tools they need to excel, be efficient, and maximize their profits.

As the world hurtles toward an AI-driven future, Dr. Raya recognizes the immense potential of ChatGPT and similar technologies. This book delves into the ways AI can revolutionize the way we do business. Dr. Raya also addresses the concerns about AI and ChatGPT. He acknowledges its limitations and is sympathetic to the skeptical entrepreneur. This book not only offers pragmatic strategies for implementing ChatGPT, enhancing efficiency, gaining competitive advantage, and optimizing costs, but it also gives advice on how to integrate AI ethically and morally.

This book also includes quotes from various entrepreneurs and small business owners who share various thoughts regarding AI, ChatGPT, and the future of small business. Their insights represent the genuine curiosity, excitement, and skepticism all entrepreneurs share. We encourage you to keep these conversations and questions in your communities as our society embraces this new technology.

"Embracing ChatGPT for Business Success" is a valuable resource for business owners looking to understand how to harness the potential of ChatGPT to gain an advantage in the competitive business world. The book hopes to be an inspiring beacon for small business owners navigating the ever-changing seas of entrepreneurship, providing them with the knowledge and tools to chart a course toward a brighter future.

To the utmost success of Doing Business Right,

DBR Publishing

INTRODUCTION

Mark started his career as a corporate employee and did that for three years. As time passed, he felt the urge to do his own thing—become his own boss to control his income and time. He put in long hours to start his venture and created marvelous products. Despite his dedication, his enterprise collapsed within a year, joining the 18.4% of businesses that don't make it to their first birthdays (Zhou, 2023). Why did Mark's business fail so quickly despite his undying entrepreneurship spirit and hard work?

The primary issue for Mark's venture that also affects the majority of small businesses that fail is a lack of resources: not enough time, lack of staffing, insufficient funds, and the struggle to keep up with competitors and evolving customer demands. With these multiple challenges, small businesses have the odds stacked against them. When you add the fact that often the owner has to perform multiple business functions—customer service, financial planning and analysis, marketing, business analytics, and sales—it can be hard to generate enough revenues and profits.

To successfully perform those functions, you need a lot of time and skills. Big companies circumvent these challenges by hiring staff for each business function. For instance, a big business typically has customer support, production, logistics, finance and accounting, marketing and sales, and information technology teams. If a small business tried to emulate large corporations and hire such staff, it wouldn't even operate for a single day before running out of funds.

Large businesses started small, the same way as you're doing. The good news is that there is one tool that can make all the difference to your business that some large companies didn't have—artificial intelligence (AI). This tool stayed under the radar for decades until OpenAI launched a chatbot called ChatGPT in November 2022. Chances are, you grabbed this book because you've detected a glimmer of hope in the midst of the struggles your business is enduring. For example, you might be working long hours, are exhausted, or your business isn't growing, and you see a chance to turn around your venture. AI and ChatGPT can help you do that by saving you time and effort and reducing business expenses.

It shouldn't surprise you that 49% of U.S. companies use ChatGPT (Bilan, 2023). Which business owner wouldn't want to cut expenses by adopting this technology? Yet, many small business owners and entrepreneurs are skeptical about AI and ChatGPT. They doubt whether ChatGPT can cater to their industry and specific business needs, have a positive impact on their businesses, and believe they'll need to have advanced technical skills beyond their grasp. Other concerns they have are that it requires a significant financial investment for AI and ChatGPT adoption and implementation, that the learning curve is too steep, or that their employees may resist AI and ChatGPT adoption.

If you have the fears mentioned above and business challenges, this book will help you overcome them. It'll also come in handy if you have troubles like these:

- **Time-consuming content creation:** You find it challenging to consistently produce high-quality content for marketing while managing other aspects of your business.
- **Legal and ethical dilemmas:** With the growing importance of data, you also worry about navigating the complex world of legal regulations around data and customer privacy.
- **Time-consuming communication:** You juggle numerous business communications and struggle to respond promptly.

- **Content creation challenges:** You struggle to create consistent and engaging content for marketing, social media, and customer support.
- **Data overload:** You have difficulty analyzing and deriving insights from large volumes of business data from your website, email marketing software, accounting software, social media, and customer relationship management (CRM) tools. You leave this data unused, akin to wasting your data collection efforts.
- **Personalization pressure:** You struggle to provide personalized customer experiences in a rapidly evolving digital landscape.
- **Resource limitations:** You're finding it tough to balance limited resources while aiming for efficient business operations.

Any entrepreneur or business owner looking to make their small business more innovative and efficient will find value in this book. It shows how you can use ChatGPT and other AI technology to save time, make money, and get ahead without software development and similar technical skills. You'll learn a simple, step-by-step process to integrate ChatGPT into various aspects of the business. Some business functions you can automate include customer service, content creation, and data analysis, all of which can save time and money.

This book is not just another tech guide; it's a hands-on manual tailored for small businesses like yours. Not only does it focus on various business aspects, but it also dives into the history of AI and how to use ChatGPT in social media marketing, lead generation and sales, and data analysis. Plus, it addresses skepticism head-on, with real-life examples and simple steps to try AI safely.

After implementing the techniques and insights from this book, you can expect to see increased operational efficiency, lower costs, and improved customer engagement. These improvements will enable you to focus more on strategic growth rather than day-to-day tasks, thereby achieving a more balanced life and a more profitable business.

Before AI and ChatGPT, it was hard to transform a small business without consulting expensive experts. In some cases, you needed large in-house teams and complex software to achieve a fraction of what AI and ChatGPT can do. For example, just hiring a good copywriter to write a single website page costs could cost anywhere from $25,000, depending on the type of content, page length, and topic. Producing an effective email could require you to spend as much as $2,000 (WebFX, n.d.). Imagine how much it would cost if you wanted five website pages and an email sequence consisting of five emails!

AI and ChatGPT can help you write compelling website pages, blog posts, emails, and other content for a fraction of the cost. Also, you could complete your writing in minutes instead of days and weeks.

These potential benefits all sound good and well, but do AI and ChatGPT *really* work? Take the story of João F. Santos, who built a T-shirt company that sold about 286 units in just five days. Santos "hired" ChatGPT as the CEO of his startup while he became its assistant. His job was to execute all the instructions that ChatGPT provided, even if they sounded risky. At that time, the t-shirt startup didn't even have a name.

Santos settled for the name AIsthetic Apparel, which ChatGPT suggested, and decided to sell T-shirts. ChatGPT also created a business plan that required starting a print-on-demand online store partnered with Printful for T-shirt printing and fulfillment of orders. Santos raised $2,500 in startup capital in exchange for a 25% share of AIsthetic Apparel. In the first five days of operating, AIsthetic Apparel sold $10,500 worth of T-shirts at $37 apiece (Nucleus_AI, 2023). Santos only worked for one hour per day in his startup.

You, too, can benefit from ChatGPT and AI as Santos did. The step you have taken in reading this book has moved you closer to building a business whose revenues and profits you can be proud of. This book is a roadmap designed for your specific needs and challenges, and by following it, you're setting yourself up for unprecedented success.

1

CHATGPT AND THE BASICS OF ARTIFICIAL INTELLIGENCE

"I was nervous about this new technology, but as I learn how to use it as a new tool for my small business, it excites me."

— SINDI M., SE CONSULTING NWA

ChatGPT isn't just a run-of-the-mill tool like virtual assistants that provide customer support online; it's like having a multi-skilled, versatile, and highly effective employee. Instead of being adept in only one business function, this employee can efficiently handle a myriad of tasks. While this is true, this dynamic employee has limitations you should know to extract maximum value from them. This chapter delves into a technological innovation behind ChatGPT known as artificial intelligence (AI) and the basics of ChatGPT, including its history and what it can and can't do for small businesses.

WHAT IS AI?

AI is the use of software to mimic human intelligence. One aspect of a person's intelligence is reason, which enables you to rationalize and make decisions. AI can "think" and "decide" the best action to reach a given goal. For example, when used in a car, it can collect the surrounding information and decide where to turn the vehicle left or right. AI can do this because it automatically learns and adapts as it gathers continuous information.

AI systems can perform human thinking functions such as writing content, coding, playing games, and interpreting speech. They achieve this by dissecting large amounts of data to identify patterns and make decisions. Some AI systems can do these functions without human intervention, while others rely on people for learning and decision-making.

A Brief History of AI

AI has a rich history and can take reams of pages to cover it fully. While it has recently become popular, AI is still a young discipline. The term "artificial intelligence" dates back to the mid-1950s at a conference to create machines that could mimic human intelligence. The need to create human-like-functioning machines was accelerated by the demands noticed during World War II. In those early days, computers were simple and could solve simpler problems by using rule-based systems. This limited the growth of AI as it required larger computing power to solve complex real-world problems.

In the late 1980s and early 1990s, decreased funds slowed down the development of AI. This period is known as the "AI winter." Despite this, research continued in areas like expert systems and natural language processing that would play a massive role later in AI development.

The tide turned for the better again for AI development in the late 1990s and early 2000s. This was when computing power increased and machine learning advanced, leading to breakthroughs in fields such as data analysis and speech recognition. This period culminated with the development of Watson—a natural language processing (NLP) computer that beat two former Jeopardy champions. It was around that time that Apple launched Siri, an AI-powered digital assistant for devices running Apple's operating systems (Tableau, n.d.).

AI continues to evolve significantly as technology keeps on advancing. This evolution is driven by the availability of massive amounts of data and deep learning for the training of AI models. Our lives are changing by leaps and bounds in many areas, including autonomous vehicles, recommendation systems, healthcare diagnostics, and virtual assistants. With the many positives, AI also demands ethical considerations for proper application.

Five AI Use Cases

AI has developed to a point where humans can use it in many applications. Some use cases include:

1. **Marketing**: AI can perform marketing functions like content creation, ad optimization, and personalized communication. With little experience, small businesses can produce marketing collateral that maximizes profits.
2. **Customer service:** AI virtual assistants and chatbots can understand customer questions and provide appropriate answers. This can remove barriers that prevent customers from buying, thereby helping increase revenues and profits.
3. **Accounting and finance:** AI can perform functions like bookkeeping, fraud detection, and invoice processing. The reduced errors in bookkeeping and invoicing coupled with decreased fraud help to maximize profits.
4. **Inventory management and logistics:** AI can come in handy with your supply chain management and improve logistics efficiencies. It can forecast demand accurately and optimize inventory and delivery routes. This leads to reduced supply chain costs and delivery times.

5. **Autonomous vehicles:** These vehicles self-navigate to reach their destinations. They scan the surroundings, map routes, and decide what to do next. When these vehicles work effectively, they expect to minimize collisions and air pollution.

BREAKING DOWN CHATGPT

ChatGPT, Chat Generative Pre-training Transformer in full, is an AI assistant that responds to your prompts. It's the brainchild of Sam Altman, who co-founded OpenAI. ChatGPT was publicly launched in November 2022. Within two months of launching, ChatGPT amassed 100 million active users, breaking TikTok's record of reaching the same milestone in nine months (Hu, 2023). Businesses of all kinds, small or large, use ChatGPT to perform multitudes of functions quickly and cost-effectively.

As people interact with ChatGPT, developers fine-tune its language-based model to make it more accurate. The larger the data set ChatGPT receives, the more it learns and can provide more accurate answers and dialogues. Other than when developers fine-tune ChatGPT, it's primarily left unsupervised when it works.

ChatGPT currently has two popular language models: GPT-3.5 and GPT-4. GPT-3.5 is fast for basic everyday tasks, and it's the free version. At the same time, GPT-4 is faster and handles more complex tasks such as advanced data analysis. You access GPT-4 when you purchase a monthly subscription to ChatGPT Plus.

You can use ChatGPT for an enormous number of tasks; only you can limit what you do with it. Some tasks it can accomplish include writing content, summarizing books or texts, and translating languages. Let's briefly expand on what this tool can do for businesses:

1. **It can generate ideas for new products or services.** If you're looking for new product or service ideas, ChatGPT can be of great help. You can ask it to give you a list of best-selling products or services in your industry or niche to kick off your search. It also allows you to drill further into each idea to learn more.

2. **It can be your content creator or copywriter.** Improved communication is vital for the success of your business, and ChatGPT can assist you with this. ChatGPT can create effective internally and externally bound emails. It can also polish our emails, making them more engaging. ChatGPT can also be a lifesaver when it comes to content generation. It can craft search-engine-optimized blog posts, newsletters, and social media posts to enhance your brand and attract customers.

3. **It can perform market research.** Conducting market research to understand your target audience's interests, desires, pains, and fears is

crucial for building a successful business. It's also worth understanding your competitors to position yourself advantageously. ChatGPT can help perform this task so that you can improve your market share, garner more customers, and retain the current ones. It achieves this task by analyzing your customer data, including their social media interactions and search engine queries.

4. **It can be your personal assistant.** ChatGPT can perform administrative tasks such as email management, scheduling tasks, and data entry. If you can free yourself from these tasks, you can focus on core business activities. Not only can ChatGPT save you time, but it can also improve efficiencies.

5. **It can help with sales.** Irrespective of which stage of the sales funnel your customers are in, ChatGPT can help you move them further down. For instance, you can use data from your virtual assistants to understand your customers and tailor your messaging to them.

6. **It can provide customer support.** When appropriately trained, ChatGPT can answer customer complaints and queries related to various issues, including shipping, billing, or product quality. This will help keep customers buying and increase revenues while reducing customer support costs.

7. **It can answer frequently asked questions (FAQs) on your website.** You can train your ChatGPT to answer FAQs accurately. This will prevent having a massive list of questions on your FAQ page while enhancing engagement. Instant answers will make your website visitors feel valued, and they'll likely do business with you, increasing your revenues.

8. **It can craft position-tailored interview questions.** You can use ChatGPT to come up with interview questions regarding your vacancy quicker than you can do so alone. The questions created might be better quality than you can craft since ChatGPT has a large amount of data to work with.

9. **It can provide personal guidance.** Many students welcome personalized help when studying complex topics. Course providers can use ChatGPT to offer detailed explanations of tough questions students ask. It can tailor these explanations to each student. You can also have ChatGPT summarize and explain touch concepts, making learning more accessible. This will allow you to reduce your staff and may lead to decreased costs, thereby maximizing profits.

10. **It can write code.** ChatGPT can help write code, reducing the time it takes to complete this task from numerous weeks to days. ChatGPT understands various programming languages,

including JavaScript and Python. Besides writing code, it can also break down how its code works and even debug it when it doesn't produce the desired results.

ChatGPT can perform a lot more tasks and save time and money. The applications of interest will depend on your business's needs. It's important to remember that this AI tool could be better and requires your input to make its outputs more accurate and relevant. While thinking about the above tasks, which ones appeal to you and why?

THE IMPORTANCE OF AI AND CHATGPT FOR SMALL BUSINESSES

Many giant corporations have made significant strides in implementing AI and ChatGPT. Still, small businesses can also benefit from these tools. AI and ChatGPT are essential for small businesses, considering the challenges they face daily. They can help you address issues like these:

- **Scaling:** In the US, more than 27 million small businesses are run by a single person, usually the owner, with no other employee (Main, 2022). Considering that this individual has to run operations, do administrative tasks, prepare financial statements and analyze them, troubleshoot business problems, provide customer support, and other key business activities, scaling their business can be a big issue. Implementing AI and ChatGPT can free time for the business owner to focus on the more essential tasks of business, which will allow them to scale their business.

- **Lack of access to top talent:** Hiring the best talent comes at a significant cost. Recruiting an $8 per hour employee can cost as much as $3,800 (Mueller, 2022). When you add the employee wage or salary, the total cost can run to more than $12,000 in the first year. Imagine how much it'd cost you if you wanted to hire top professionals in fields like software development, data science, logistics, or bookkeeping! Introducing AI and ChatGPT can take up some of these roles and save you the cost of hiring top talent. You can hire low-salary employees, train them on your ChatGPT integrations, and produce quality work at a lower cost.

- **Delivering unmatched customer support:** Due to a lack of resources, small businesses struggle with delighting their customers. Some have issues to reach their desired customer satisfaction rates. With AI and ChatGPT, you can automate customer support and deliver timely customer support almost any time of the day. In turn, you'll increase your customer retention rates and lower your customer acquisition costs, which will improve your profits.

- **Landing enough customers:** While retaining customers is good, your business revenue may plateau due to a lack of new buyers. To attract these customers, you need effective marketing and sales. The lack of top marketing and sales talent may stand in your way, which is where AI and ChatGPT can come to your rescue. These tools can help you craft marketing and sales materials that not only match your brand voice, tone, and style but can also convert leads into customers cost-effectively.

- **Accurate financial planning:** It's almost a cliché that numerous small businesses suffocate due to poor cash flow or lack of capital. At the root of these troubles lurks the real struggle of having an accurate financial plan. AI and ChatGPT may not create this kind of plan for you, but they can help with financial analysis from your financial data. They can also provide actionable insights you can factor into your financial plan and improve its quality and accuracy.

If you could use AI and ChatGPT to address one of the above challenges in your business, your life wouldn't be the same again.

HOW TO START SMALL

Implementing AI and ChatGPT is a process to be approached with care. Mistakes can be costly, but their impact can be minimized if you start small. There is a step-by-step process to consider following:

- **Survey your customers.** Whether your business is a startup or established, surveying your customers can improve revenue. This also allows you to begin using AI. Select an AI-powered survey software such as Holler, Typeform, or Blocksurvey and create a survey to understand your customers' needs. These tools come with reporting and analytics you can use to analyze the needs of your customers.
- **Use AI-powered market research tools to learn more about your customers.** The customer survey responses are helpful but insufficient because people can act contrary to what they say. That's why you need to use other sources of information to provide customer insights. AI-powered tools such as Pecan, Brandwatch, and Crayon can analyze data from social media and search engines to understand customer insights.
- **Develop a customer avatar.** Use the above data to understand your customers' needs and create a customer avatar. Having a customer avatar allows you to target prospective customers by using their

needs and preferences. This means you can improve prospect-to-customer conversions and reach a wider audience.

- **Estimate revenues and profits.** When you understand the needs of your potential customers, you can figure out what product or service to create. Before creating that product or service, it's worth ensuring that your business will make enough money. Calculate revenues you can generate based on a conservative estimated number of sales. Estimate your expenses for creating, selling, and distributing your product or service. Subtract the total expenses from sales to determine if creating a new product or service will be profitable. If it's not profitable, you may need to consider a new product or service. The process we've suggested works even when you want to expand the sales of your existing product or service.

- **Test the market-product fit.** Market your product or service to your target customers. If you make sales profitably, you will have validated your AI-driven strategy for meeting customer needs.

The above process is just one way of leveraging AI and proving to yourself the enormous benefits of this technology. If AI works on a small project, it'll work on a larger one, allowing you to scale your business quickly. The good news is that you'll do this without incurring excessive costs, thus maximizing profits.

FINANCIAL IMPLICATIONS OF IMPLEMENTING AI AND CHATGPT

If you knew that implementing a particular business decision would lose you money, would you do it? Of course, you wouldn't because you want your business to maximize profits. The same thinking should apply when you consider AI and ChatGPT implementation. That's why you need to conduct a cost-benefit analysis of introducing AI and ChatGPT into your enterprise; this chapter provides a simplified illustration of how to do this.

Let's assume you run a successful e-commerce business; you want to decide whether to implement AI and Chat-GPT-based customer support into your company. Note that the figures used are all fictitious and merely for illustrative purposes.

The first part of your cost-benefit analysis examines the benefits of implementing AI and ChatGPT. Implementing AI and ChatGPT increases customer satisfaction by 15%, reducing the customer churn rate by 10%. The estimated annual increase in revenue due to improved customer support is $100,000. Your AI and ChatGPT are so effective you don't see the need to keep five of your customer support agents. This results in estimated labor cost savings of $150,000 per year.

AI and ChatGPT decrease customer inquiry response times and allow your business to handle 20% more customer inquiries. More customers decide to stay with your business, which results in a theoretical $50,000 increased revenue annually. Interactions with customers provide better data insights, leading to improved marketing strategies and an additional $30,000 in annual revenue. The data insights also help you understand your customer better, leading to the creation of an accurate customer avatar. Your sales generation efforts increase the number and quality of leads, and revenue skyrockets by another $40,000 annually.

AI and ChatGPT also enable you to deliver consistent customer support and messaging and save $10,000 annually due to errors and misunderstandings. This brings the total dollar benefits to $380,000 ($100,000 + $150,000 + $ 50,000 + $30,000 + $40,000 + $10,000 = $380,000).

Of course, the above benefits come with certain costs. The major one is developing and integrating AI and ChatGPT into your business systems, which could cost $50,000. To keep your AI and ChatGPT current, you'll need to maintain and update them regularly, costing $15,000 annually. It also costs your business $20,000 annually to comply with data privacy and security.

It's prudent to anticipate adoption resistance from your employees and customers. In that regard, you estimate that educating them will cost $5,000 annually. To implement new technology, you must train your team, or you won't get the buy-in you need. For this purpose, your calculations estimate you'll spend $10,000 annually. To address technical issues, you expect to set aside $5,000 annually. The total costs for implementing AI and ChatGPT amount to $105,000 ($50,000 + $15,000 + $20,000 + $5,000 + $10,000 + $5,000 = $105,000).

The estimated profit for implementing AI and ChatGPT will be $275,000 ($380,000 - $105,000 = $275,000). This translates to an estimated ROI of 262% ($275,000/$105,000 x 100 = 262%), or for every $1 spent to implement and maintain the AI system, you expect to generate $2.62 ($105,000/$105,000 : $275,000/$105,000 = 1 : 2.62). It's rare to find such returns, and it is determined this project is worth implementing.

AI and ChatGPT can turn around the fortunes of your business. Despite their benefits, many small business owners and entrepreneurs are still skeptical. They raise questions like "Is AI safe? Is it ethical? Can I truly rely on it for building, growing, and scaling my business?" The next chapter will address these questions and more.

2

OVERCOMING AI AND CHATGPT SKEPTICISM

"I'm concerned about it removing the authenticity of writing and artistic expression."

— APRIL PELKEY, SUPERIOR MARKETING
SOLUTIONS NWA

Isabella owns a small bakery that was once skeptical about ChatGPT. Her tech-savvy friends had introduced it to her, but she couldn't believe that a chatbot could help her maximize profits and optimize efficiencies. Isabella had a challenge: She needed help with how to improve her marketing and customer service. Isabella had tried numerous tools like social media marketing tools and couldn't find one that worked well for her business.

One day, when Isabella was talking to her friend Olivia, a marketing manager at a large fintech company, ChatGPT came up. Olivia told Isabella how she had been using ChatGPT to generate creative marketing ideas and content in a fraction of the time she used to. She also spoke about how happy her clients were with her ideas and the success they saw.

Isabella remained skeptical but decided she had nothing to lose for trying ChatGPT. She created a free account and discovered how easy ChatGPT was to use. The responses she got to her queries from ChatGPT were informative. Encouraged, Isabella began to create customer support emails, blog posts, and social marketing posts with ChatGPT. Her skepticism melted when she saw her website traffic inching higher and higher and customer orders increased. What startled Isabella even more was that she accomplished her marketing and customer service tasks quicker.

Impressed by her results, Isabella wrote a note to her friend Olivia, saying, "As you know, I was skeptical about ChatGPT at first, but I'm so glad I tried it. It has helped skyrocket my website traffic, resulting in more customer orders while saving me a ton of time on marketing and customer service tasks. I highly recommend ChatGPT to any small business owner looking to increase their efficiencies and maximize profits."

It's okay to be skeptical about AI and ChatGPT, but you might miss grand opportunities to turn your business around and make a bundle of money while working less like Isabella. It's a good idea to understand why you're skeptical and whether that's warranted. In this chapter, we look at the myths surrounding AI and ChatGPT and address safety concerns you might have.

BREAKING DOWN AI MYTHS AND SKEPTICISM

The power of AI is taking the world by storm. Others think this tool will replace humans and there will be no jobs anymore. This fear is warranted, considering products like fully autonomous cars need no drivers. Unfortunately, the doubts and fears people have about AI have given birth to various myths, fuelling the skepticism we often hear. Skepticism means an attitude of doubt or a disposition to incredulity, either in general or toward a particular object (Merriam-Webster, n.d.).

It's worth understanding what these myths are and eliminating the doubts you have about AI. This section will help you with this by examining eight common AI myths.

1. **Myth #1—ChatGPT is effective only for big businesses.** Large businesses like OpenAI, Facebook, and Amazon dominate using AI-powered tools. Of course, these giant businesses have massive budgets and skills to maximize the

use of these tools. This perception leads many small business owners to think that tools like ChatGPT can't be helpful for them. The reality is that ChatGPT can be useful for all kinds of businesses, from small to medium-sized to mega companies. All businesses need to perform certain functions to thrive, including operations, marketing, logistics or distribution, and human resources. If a mega business can use ChatGPT to provide top customer support, a small company can do the same. The difference will often be that the large company will do it on a bigger scale than the smaller business. So, ChatGPT levels the playing field, making it possible for small businesses, including solopreneurs, to compete with conglomerates.

2. **Myth #2—ChatGPT is self-aware.** ChatGPT can indeed converse like a human being, making it look like it has a mind. The architecture of this tool mimics the human brain functions, but it doesn't have a mind and can't be self-aware. It relies on information and the rules developers set to perform its functions. ChatGPT can't think for itself—while it may resemble a real person with feelings, it is just an advanced computer that processes information.

3. **Myth #3—I don't need ChatGPT in my business.** A business can thrive without ChatGPT, and enterprises have done so for hundreds of years.

Understandably, you might not need ChatGPT. The truth is that today's business landscape has become challenging, making it tough to compete. Not adopting tools like ChatGPT may prevent your business from grabbing the massive opportunities this technology brings. Instead of maximizing profits by minimizing costs, your business may do the opposite. You don't have to adopt ChatGPT in all your business processes. You can start with one area, say marketing, and progressively introduce it to other business functions.

4. **Myth #4—ChatGPT is never wrong.** ChatGPT provides human-like responses to questions and prompts, and it seems to be spot-on all the time. The information that ChatGPT uses is currently up-to-date until 2021. If you ask it a question whose answer requires knowledge from 2022, it will not return an accurate answer. For instance, I asked it to tell me what's Amazon's bestselling non-fiction in 2023, and it got it wrong. Besides, ChatGPT tends to provide more accurate information when asked simple questions or prompts. While information is continually updated on ChatGPT, it's essential to fact-check the responses you get from this tool.

5. **Myth #5—ChatGPT will eliminate human collaboration.** Interpersonal communication doesn't only involve the exchange of speech;

people also communicate non-verbally, which ChatGPT can't do because it has no emotions or thoughts as humans do. ChatGPT is technically an invisible robot, making it more suitable to perform tasks within restricted boundaries. You can expect human collaboration to still be vital in expressing feelings and expression.

6. **Myth #6—ChatGPT will replace your employees.** While ChatGPT can do routine tasks such as writing code, handling customer queries, and producing content, it doesn't replace your employees. The design of ChatGPT was not to replace your staff but to help improve their efficiency on time-consuming and repetitive work.

7. **Myth #7—ChatGPT renders training and onboarding unnecessary.** Implementing ChatGPT improves employee and business efficiencies but doesn't eliminate training and onboarding. New employees will still need training and onboarding to ensure they understand how to use ChatGPT effectively. To ensure continued process improvement, it's worth training your hires on how you integrated ChatGPT. These new eyes may identify opportunities you have never considered when integrating this tool into your business systems.

8. **Myth #8—ChatGPT instantly improves your business's performance.** Some tasks, such as

writing content and sales copy, will happen faster when you use ChatGPT. This content doesn't necessarily mean these efficiencies will cause an instant improvement in your business's performance. It can take a while as you fine-tune and adapt your AI technology to your business needs for this to occur. Have realistic expectations and patience when you adopt ChatGPT.

The above myths indicate that ChatGPT is a business tool like your computer. It's not meant to replace you or your employees but to complement your work. With the proper ChatGPT perspective, you can adopt it where necessary and for good reasons.

SAFETY IN AI

Some people believe individuals can use AI to steal personal information. This concern doesn't only apply to AI but also to any online application, such as a website. Many of these tools, including AI and ChatGPT, are safe to use, provided you don't share sensitive information with them. OpenAI has implemented security measures to ensure users are safe using this tool. It's essential to understand these measures and comply with the requirements for your protection. Before we explore two security interventions that OpenAI has implemented, let's look at the risks of using ChatGPT.

ChatGPT comes with two crucial risks you need to understand and accept: ChatGPT collects your personal information when you open an account, and the dialogues you have with it are not fully confidential. Let's first discuss the risk of collecting personal data.

Like most online applications, ChatGPT gathers your personal data such as your location, email address, phone number, and name when you open an account, share this information on OpenAI's social media accounts, or include it in your prompts or file uploads. The risks associated with this include the possibility it may fall into the wrong hands. Fortunately, OpenAI promises that it will not sell this information to third parties. Keep in mind, however, that this data could land in the hands of OpenAI's affiliates and service providers without your knowledge. Importantly, you'll know when OpenAI updates its privacy policy.

The dialogues and information you provide are stored and used by default to fine-tune ChatGPT. This stored data means that OpenAI's developers can view the information you provide (OpenAI, 2023). You can't be sure what these developers will do with that information. That's why it's crucial to avoid sharing sensitive information—information the user wants to keep private—with ChatGPT.

Despite the abovementioned risks, OpenAI has taken steps to enhance your information security when using

ChatGPT. It's time to examine two categories of measures created for this purpose: security and data handling.

ChatGPT's Security Measures

We understand the importance of being secure when using ChatGPT, and OpenAI feels the same. That's why it put security measures in place to guard your information on its servers, including the following:

- **External security audits:** Not only does the OpenAI have internal audits in place, but it also hires external security auditors to perform penetration testing. This test aims to identify and fix vulnerabilities to protect user data.
- **Compliance with local, regional, and international personal data policies:** The GDPR, applicable in the EU, requires OpenAI to get permission before collecting its users' personal data. In contrast, California's CCPA demands that OpenAI allow users to opt out of its data collection practices. SOC 2 Type 2 charges OpenAI to stay on top of security and privacy to protect its users' data.
- **Data encryption and access controls:** Data encryption, at rest and when transferred between systems, ensures your data is protected. This prevents unauthorized access. Coupled with data encryption is access control to safeguard

unauthorized people from accessing OpenAI's customer data.

- **Bug bounty program:** This program rewards security researchers and ethical hackers for helping keep OpenAI's technology safe and secure for its users. All it takes is to report security issues or vulnerabilities you find in OpenAI's technology. It's managed by Bugcrowd, one of the leading bug bounty platforms.

The above initiatives indicate that OpenAI is committed to protecting its customers' data.

Data Handling Processes

OpenAI knows how crucial its customers' data is, so it has practices to protect their data. Unless it does this, its users won't trust it and will likely take their business to competitors. Here are some data handling practices that OpenAI uses.

- **It extends certain rights to users.** OpenAI grants you certain statutory rights that may link with your location. These rights may include deleting, updating, or accessing your personal information. You may also withdraw your consent for OpenAI to process your data.
- **It may share your data with third parties.** OpenAI may share your data with third parties under certain circumstances. For instance, your

data could be shared for legal reasons such as to protect OpenAI's products and services, if mandated by law, or in case OpenAI is sold. Luckily, OpenAI will ensure those third parties adhere to the same level of privacy and data handling processes.

- **It's transparent regarding the collection of personal information.** OpenAI collects personal information to enhance ChatGPT and related services and improve the user experience. Other significant reasons for gathering this information include to abide by the law and for security purposes.

- **It retains your personal information when it's necessary to do so.** OpenAI promises to keep your personal data for as long as it provides services like ChatGPT. The length of time it retains this information will depend on its nature, risk of disclosure, or legal reasons.

The above practices are a testament that OpenAI is committed to protecting its customers' data. We should point out that the security of your personal information on ChatGPT doesn't only depend on OpenAI because you have a role to play. Understanding OpenAI's security and privacy policies is crucial to abide by them and improve your data protection.

PRACTICAL STEPS TO SAFELY EMBRACE AI

Implementing AI in your business appears complex and scary. It doesn't have to be that way if you consider what we'll share with you below. Not only will this simplify and make the implementation cost-effective, but it'll also help you use AI and ChatGPT safely. Let's first consider the steps you can take to integrate AI and ChatGPT into your business:

- **Evaluate your current business tasks.** Categorize your business activities in terms of areas like production, operations, marketing and sales, finance, information technology, and logistics. For each category, make a list of repetitive tasks that your business accomplishes.
- **Prioritize the tasks you can automate with AI and ChatGPT.** List the tasks from the highest to the least priority regarding automation. Choose two or three of the top-priority tasks to automate with AI and ChatGPT.
- **Determine your AI and ChatGPT implementation goals.** For each top-priority task, set your implementation goal. Your goals will help you decide which AI tools to pick.
- **Pick the right AI tools.** There's a massive list of AI tools, making it crucial to select the right applications. Go for AI tools that will enable you to achieve your goals. For instance, if your goal is

to enhance customer service, you could select a chatbot.

- **Pilot your AI implementation.** As stated earlier, it's helpful to start small when incorporating AI into your business. This is the time to collect data, and feedback from your team and customers will allow you to fine-tune your applications cost-effectively before scaling. Once your AI works as you want, you can scale its implementation.

As you go through the above-mentioned steps, pay attention to the safe implementation of AI and ChatGPT. The checklist below provides safety best practices to consider when using AI tools:

1. **Verify and validate your AI systems.** It's paramount to verify, validate, and test your AI systems for robustness and safety before implementing them.
2. **Train your employees on the proper use of your AI tools.** Educate your employees on AI usage best practices, potential risks, and quick reporting of suspicious activity.
3. **Avoid exposing sensitive information to your AI software.** This will prevent sensitive information from being stolen due to data breaches.

4. **Update yourself on AI risks regularly.** You need to stay updated on best practices and security concerns to remain protected.

5. **Develop rules and regulations for AI usage.** To ensure ethical use of your AI systems, create guidelines for their safe use. Include ethical considerations to ensure your AI systems are used for the right reasons, and your customers and personnel trust them.

6. **Consider using premium AI tools.** Paid AI tools often provide more robust security features and reliability than their free counterparts. You could start with free versions but migrate to premium ones before scaling.

7. **Secure all data handled by your AI systems.** Implement a robust authentication system and data handling processes and policies to prevent malicious actors from accessing your AI information.

8. **Check for plagiarism and copyright infringement in your AI-generated content.** Use processes like plagiarism checkers to verify that content generated by your AI systems isn't plagiarized. Another thing that's worth protecting against is copyright infringement.

Hopefully, we have addressed some of the skepticism you had about AI and ChatGPT before reading this chapter. The key takeaway is that any business can use AI tools, but make sure you secure your information and that of your vendors and customers.

It's now time to think about business areas where you can use AI tools, such as logistics, customer support, and email marketing. Before implementing AI, make sure that you have a written plan on how you're going to protect your business's data and that of your vendors and customers.

Having covered the foundational theory about AI and ChatGPT, it's time to apply what you've learned to enhance your customer service.

3

BOOSTING CUSTOMER SERVICE

"...this new AI sounds very futuristic. This can break new ground for the world.

...can this create communication problems?"

— ERNIE R., SE CONSULTING NWA

W hat if there was a way to respond to every customer inquiry instantly, any time of the day, without running multiple shifts? Imagine the impact on your sales, customer experiences, and customer service costs! You don't have to imagine doing this because ChatGPT can help make this happen. It takes learning how to use this tool for this purpose, and this chapter will guide you. You'll also learn about the multiple customer support benefits you'll enjoy by employing AI and ChatGPT.

AUTOMATING CUSTOMER SUPPORT WITH CHATGPT

Emily is a customer service representative for a growing e-commerce enterprise called SmartShopper. Known for lightning-quick deliveries and superb customer service, SmartShopper went into expansion faster than the owners thought. With this expansion, customer complaints, queries, and questions increased.

On a particular day, Emily's day began as usual. She donned her headset, perched herself on her seat, and readied herself to provide customer support like her colleagues. Emails flooded the customer service inbox while, at the same time, phones buzzed to no end with customer-related issues. As Emily's day progressed, the number of customer queries crept up exponentially. No matter how quickly Emily responded to those queries, more kept coming. Emily felt like she was drowning in customer complaints and questions, as did her fellow agents. Customers were left fuming and waiting hours before somebody addressed their concerns. Smart-Shopper was understaffed, and this led to slow response times.

Three issues were responsible for this: Emily couldn't provide real-time customer engagements, some of her agents were rude, and she transferred some concerns to more competent agents. Some of SmartShopper's customers sprang to social media to vent their frustrations.

As the business day drew to a close, Emily became deflated; she had done her best to help customers, but she fell short of expectations numerous times. During the period of less-than-stellar customer support, the business received a fair share of negative reviews, lost many customers, and its reputation declined. Fortunately, SmartShopper's management identified and overhauled the troubles with the company's customer support operations. The revamp improved SmartShpper's customer service and regained some of its lost customers, improving its bottom line.

Your business could be in the same boat as SmartShopper, facing a customer decline due to a can-improve customer support. You can turn this around by resorting to ChatGPT and injecting life into your profits. This section will discuss how to do this.

How to Use ChatGPT for Simple and Repetitive Customer Service Tasks

Using ChatGPT to automate repetitive customer service tasks improves consistency, saves time, reduces costs, and enhances scalability. All these benefits can maximize revenues and profits while improving customer service efficiencies. It's essential to properly implement

ChatGPT to enjoy those benefits, and here's how you do this:

1. **Step #1—Discover common customer issues.** Customers' issues are often the same regarding a given product or service. You can find out customers' common questions by asking for feedback, speaking with your customer service team, or reviewing support tickets. Studying your direct competitors may also reveal customer concerns you may have not thought about. Consider asking ChatGPT for ideas about your customers' concerns.

2. **Step #2—Generate training data for your ChatGPT model.** A ChatGPT model is an AI-powered and automated tool for handling business activities such as customer service and lead generation. Turn all the customer concerns you have into frequently asked questions (FAQs) and provide answers to those questions. You can also use other customer service documents, such as customer support scripts, product documents, and transcripts, to ensure you capture all typical customer concerns. Feed all this data into your ChatGPT model so that it knows what to look for and how to respond. This book doesn't specify the setup, as different models exist. We provide a broader overview of when you've selected and worked to implement the AI model

into your business and discover how ChatGPT can help.

3. **Step #3—Create your ChatGPT model.** Use the training data generated above to create your ChatGPT model. Fine-tune your model by adjusting its parameters so that it provides accurate customer support concerning common issues and that it can address them.

4. **Step #4—Test your ChatGPT model.** Take your fine-tuned ChatGPT model for a test run to make sure that it provides excellent customer support. You can get your customer support team to interact with your model and give feedback for further fine-tuning it.

5. **Step #5—Integrate your ChatGPT model into your customer support system.** One of the ways to achieve this is by installing an automated chatbot. Alternatively, you can provide your customer support team access to your ChatGPT model to help handle some customer queries.

The above five-step process for using ChatGPT simplifies automating your customer support services. When implemented, you can expect to save time and costs, improve efficiencies, and enhance your customer support's consistency. Companies like HelloFresh from the US and Octopus Energy from the UK have successfully used AI tools to provide customer support and see amazing results. Let's briefly discover how HelloFresh leveraged AI to streamline its customer support operations and win big.

HelloFresh offers ingredients for home-cooked meals in exchange for a monthly subscription fee. Facing slow response times, a frustrated customer service team, and the need to monitor incoming Facebook messages, it turned to AI for help. This transition led to the birth of a chatbot named Freddy that can reply to users, recommend music, and provide content during public holidays. Once implemented, Freddy reduced the average time to respond to a customer query from five hours to one hour and 11 minutes—the equivalent of a 76% improvement in response time. It's exciting that HelloFresh achieved these results despite receiving 47% more messages than before the implementation of Freddy (Rybakova, 2022). This freed the customer support team from doing simple and repetitive customer support tasks and allowed more focus on more complex inquiries.

When leveraging AI and ChatGPT, remember that ChatGPT has limitations. For example, it can't handle complex and unique customer inquiries or may be unable to provide support in a language it wasn't trained in.

THE ADVANTAGES YOU DIDN'T KNOW YOU NEEDED

In 2022, Zendesk (a software-as-a-service Danish-American company) dissected data from a survey that spanned

21 countries, thousands of customers, and customer service people to help businesses avoid making customer service mistakes. Not only did it discover that customer service directly impacts a business's performance, but it also found the following:

- eighty-nine percent of customers will spend more if you provide answers online without them talking to any person
- ninety percent of the customers spend more if you provide personalized customer service
- ninety-two percent will spend more if they don't have to repeat what they say when they get customer service

What's worrying is that 30% of the customer agents feel disempowered to perform their jobs. When you consider that 76% of customers want an immediate response when they contact your company, there's a chance they may not have a positive experience. One bad experience is enough for the customer to take their money to your competitors (Zendesk, n.d.).

Most of the above customer preferences can be handled by the proper application of AI and ChatGPT. We must reemphasize that the customer service benefits you get from ChatGPT are available to your enterprise, even if it's a one-person operation. Some of the benefits you may enjoy are as follows:

- **Enhanced customer satisfaction:** A business that employs automated customer support can achieve about 90% customer satisfaction rates (Sidor, 2023). Reasons for this include the fact that you can set up automated customer service to provide personalized assistance. There's no need to interact with a customer agent, and customers give details of their concerns once. We can't overlook the impact of reduced response times and faster resolution of customer inquiries.

- **Improved revenues and profits:** By automating your customer services, your business can shave up to 50% of this area's costs (Sidor, 2023). Besides saving money, automated customer services can pump up your revenues. Because automatic customer support operates 24/7, it's likely to catch some customers when they're ready to buy. It can achieve this by identifying people prepared to buy and providing key features and benefits of your product or service known to convert prospects into customers. Automated customer support AI tools can also notice when your prospect gets stuck on your website and provide personalized help that may convert them into customers.

- **Reduced the burnout of customer agents:** Automating almost all repetitive customer inquiries reduces the workload of your agents. This allows them to focus on more complex issues that require human interaction. With as many as 70% of customer agents on the brink of burnout, automating customer support will be a welcome relief to them (Sidor, 2023). The absence of burnout means your agents will likely perform their tasks better, further helping improve your top and bottom lines.

- **Reduced chances for customers to repeat themselves:** As stated in the opening of this section, customers don't like repeating themselves multiple times. Unfortunately, some businesses fail to meet this need because their customer service channels operate in isolation. Automation eliminates this issue by syncing up all your customer support channels. This will boost customer experience and cater to the 80% who prefer interacting with businesses that provide consistent messages and experiences across all their channels (Sidor, 2023).

Automating your customer support will positively impact your customers, agents, and your business's revenues and profits. AI and ChatGPT can handle multiple customer service tasks. Still, they may not be suitable for handling sensitive or complex issues that require human discretion and empathy.

SAMPLE PROMPTS TO SUPERCHARGE YOUR CUSTOMER SERVICE

How can you use ChatGPT for customer service if you don't create your own model? Your best bet is to employ ChatGPT prompts tailored to resolve specific customer concerns. In this section, we'll provide real-world, practical prompts you can plug into ChatGPT and get the desired responses. Strong prompts will save you time and optimize your customer support efficiencies.

The prompts below are just examples and must be tailored to your business's and customers' needs. Before we share those prompts with you, let's first understand what a prompt is and how it works.

A prompt is a question, query, or instruction you give to ChatGPT to provide a proper response. When ChatGPT receives your prompt, it leverages its pre-trained knowledge, information, and natural language processing prowess to pop out an answer. Your prompt should be clear and specific for ChatGPT to deliver the desired response. Sometimes, it's necessary to experiment and refine your prompt for ChatGPT to churn out satisfactory answers.

Now that you know what a prompt is and how it works, let's go over different prompts tailored for delivering excellent customer support:

Prompt for Crafting Customer Surveys

Use this prompt to elicit customer opinions regarding your customer support or any other business operation. In this case, you aim to create customer surveys earmarked to improve customer experience.

One of the powerful ways of getting good responses to your prompts is to place ChatGPT in the position of your business. Let's illustrate a prompt crafted with this idea in mind.

"Imagine that you sell [product or service] through your custom website. You have recently created [innovation you've just created], and you want to know the experiences your customers have with it. The feedback your customers give will be used to improve [your innovation] for a better customer experience. Compose a short customer survey of [number of questions] to help you achieve your goal."

People don't want long surveys, or else they won't respond to your survey. Target creating a survey a person can complete in under five minutes to optimize the number of responses you receive (Cornell, 2022).

Prompt for Creating Knowledge Base Articles

Knowledge-based articles can be lifesavers for addressing customer concerns. They're designed to provide step-by-step answers or instructions for solving a specific problem. Not only do these resources help solve customer issues, but they also reduce inquiries that customer support agents have to deal with.

Here's an example of a prompt to pop into ChatGPT and get a knowledge base article you can then refine:

"Compose a knowledge base article on [a customer's concern]. Provide a step-by-step process for addressing this concern, ensuring you're empathetic toward the customer."

Prompt for Replying to Negative Reviews

Negative reviews can hurt your business's revenues, bottom line, and reputation. Nearly all consumers check reviews before purchasing, and 96% of these customers pay more attention to negative reviews. Social media reviews can convert visitors up to 40 times better than other channels (Taheer, 2023). Quicker responses to reviews might not immediately correct what went wrong, but they can minimize business damage.

Replies to negative reviews need to be prompt, professional, personal, and honest and address the concerns raised. ChatGPT not only can give empathetic responses to negative reviews, but it can also create reviews that tick all the other boxes. As we stated earlier, ChatGPT's responses will be consistent because they are not emotional like humans.

Here's an example of a prompt you can feed into ChatGPT to generate an empathetic response to a negative review:

"A customer wrote a negative review on your [website, social media platform, or search engine] for [the cause of the negative review]. Write an empathetic, personal, and professional response to such a review to manage the damage caused."

Prompt for Managing Customer Complaints or Issues

There are many reasons customers can complain between when they purchase a product or service and during its use. It's essential to handle those complaints carefully to avoid negative reviews and damage to your brand.

ChatGPT can help address and manage various customer issues, from billing errors to product delivery to product quality. You can use a prompt like the one below for this purpose:

"Suppose that you run a website that provides [type of product or service]. A customer bought a product or service you recommended, and they're complaining that it's not doing what you promised. Craft a response that addresses this problem courteously, empathetically, and professionally. Your ultimate desire is to keep this customer and persuade them to leave a positive review instead of a negative one."

Prompt for Providing Technical Support

Depending on your kind of business, it may be necessary to provide technical assistance to your customers. This is often the case if you sell technology-based products or services such as cloud services, video-creation software, or electronics.

It's advantageous to your business to provide technical support for your customers to receive the most from your products or services. This may lead to improved online reviews and increased revenues and profits.

Here's an example prompt for providing technical support:

"Your company has recently launched a website-based [product or service]. You have received [number of customer queries] regarding [the technical issue the customers are facing]. Write an empathetic and professional script that your customer service agents can use to handle this issue."

Prompts to Manage Cancellations and Refunds

This prompt aims to help your business minimize cancellations and refunds to maximize profits, especially for subscription-based businesses. A cancellation policy is good business practice, but customers may not understand it. This will require the intervention of your customer service agents.

Unfortunately, you could face too many cancellations, increasing the workload of your customer support team. ChatGPT can improve your customer service team's efficiencies and potentially minimize cancellations. A prompt like the one below will help improve the efficiency of your customer support:

"Suppose you run a [type of business and product or service it offers]. After analyzing your business, you realized that you could improve profits by [percentage improvement you require] if you reduce cancellations and refunds by [percentage desired]. Compose a fair, empathetic, professional, and persuasive customer response that helps prevent customer cancellations and refunds."

This prompt doesn't stop customers from canceling and requesting refunds; it reassures your customers that you genuinely care about them and would like an opportunity to fix what you may have done wrong.

To use the above prompt in your business, customize it with your type of business and the products or services it offers. Also, adjust the percentage of profits you could make for a given level of cancellations and refunds.

Prompts like this could also form part of your customer onboarding process to minimize cancellation requests as early as possible. Changing a customer's mind can be challenging when they've already decided to cancel and receive a refund.

Prompt to Help Address Billing and Payment Inquiries

Billing and payment queries deal with issues at the end of your sales funnel. You can't allow these issues to creep up and minimize your revenues and profits. It takes having an efficient customer support team to remove barriers that prevent customers from paying or to prevent them from even asking for refunds. Overall, prompts in this customer support category can handle issues regarding payment methods, account information, and billing statements.

A good example of a prompt to deal with a payment inquiry goes like this:

"Imagine operating a business that sells [product or service]. A customer claims they paid their bill in the previous month, but it still shows as due. Craft a reply that shows you've reviewed the customer's bill payment history and you're resolving the issue."

Of course, you'll need to customize the above prompt with your business-specific situation. As we said earlier, the more specific and clear your prompt is, the better the ChatGPT response you'll receive and optimized customer support efficiencies.

Automating your customer support will positively impact your customers, agents, and your business's revenues and profits. It's crucial to remember that AI and ChatGPT can't execute some customer support tasks like a human can. For instance, it can't be emotionally intelligent or understand the context behind a dialogue. Where you need these human qualities, you'll need to refine ChatG-PT's output accordingly.

Despite these limitations, ChatGPT is still one of this century's revolutionary technologies that's changing the provision of customer service. Its prowess doesn't stop with helping your business deliver improved customer service; ChatGPT can also help you create various types of content. The next chapter delves into how you can use this tool for efficient content creation.

4

STREAMLINED CONTENT CREATION

"...if people can learn to use ChatGPT as the tool it is, it could be a game changer for small businesses who don't have a budget for a content creator or copywriter."

— BRITT TAYLOR, THE BURNING BRA,
NONPROFIT ORGANIZATION

I magine your content process is like a river—now remove the dams and watch it flow smoothly. The dams represent the challenges that hinder the smooth flow of your content creation process. It's crucial to know what those obstacles are and where they are so that you can figure out how to remove them and free the river to flow smoothly. This chapter will help you identify the troubles you face with content creation and provide an amazing solution.

UNLOCKING CONTENT CREATION WITH CHATGPT

Content has become an integral part of many small businesses. It's not surprising that 73% of business-to-business (B2B) and 70% of business-to-consumer (B2C) companies include content in their marketing strategies (Riddall, 2023). When you consider that content marketing costs 62% less and delivers three times more leads than outbound efforts, you also have good reasons to use content marketing. The problem is that small businesses face challenges such as the following when it comes to content creation:

- **Inconsistent content generation:** The small business owner wears multiple hats to keep the wheels turning. These hats leave them with insufficient time to create quality content consistently. Failure to do this prevents you from becoming a revered thought leader in your industry. Most importantly, your business fails to rank high on search engines and struggles to attract as many customers as you'd have liked.
- **Lack of resources:** Generating quality content is more challenging because it demands skill and time. It's understandable to want to create this

content since you know your business better than anyone. You can't always do this due to a lack of time and money to hire skilled writers.

- **Increasing number of competitors:** You'll unlikely be the first to create content in your industry or niche. There are probably thousands of blogs competing for the same eyeballs. Some of your competitors have been producing content for years and are seen as authorities. With more and more people creating blogs, outperforming your competition is getting even more demanding. Your best bet to dominate is to produce more quality content. As you make quality content consistently, your audience's expectations will rise, and you'll need to keep up.

- **Producing content in multiple content formats:** Your target audience consumes content differently; some prefer text, while others enjoy consuming audio, graphics, or video. Video might be the popular content format, but it doesn't mean that's the case for your audience. To optimize reader engagement and improve your sales generation, you need to produce content in multiple formats. Again, this demands time, skills, and money you may not have.

- **Writer's block:** Nothing frustrates you as much as facing a blank page or screen and not knowing where to start with writing your content. This is often the result of having to consistently come up with fresh ideas and meet strict deadlines. Don't despair if you often face this challenge because even the most creative writers fall victim to writer's block.

- **Writing engaging content:** There's no point in producing content for the sake of it; that would be a waste of time and energy. The competition for readers or viewers is high, and there are tons of information sources. To compete, you'll need to produce unique and engaging content, which takes skill and time. For instance, you need to understand your target audience and tailor your content to their needs and wants, which requires research skills. Your content must also align with your buyer's journey to convert them into customers.

You've now identified what stands between you and your content creation efforts. ChatGPT can help you overcome many of the above challenges without hiring freelance writers. This tool can create various content, including blog posts, newsletters, social media content, case studies, press releases, and even FAQs for your website.

When you use ChatGPT, gone will be the days of taking forever to create a piece of content. Your content creation efficiency and creativity will go to another level. If you struggle with writer's block, ChatGPT can help with content research and idea generation. You can take this further and ask it to create a draft of the content you want. All this work will take a small fraction of the time you usually need to create high-quality content.

Step-by-Step Guide for Using ChatGPT to Create Different Kinds of Content

ChatGPT can be indispensable for content creation if you learn how to use it. This section covers how to use it to write various types of content, such as blog posts, press releases, email content, and social media content.

How to Create a Blog Post With ChatGPT

It can be time-consuming to create a blog the traditional way. ChatGPT shortens this process, allowing you to quickly post your articles to your website and attract visitors. Crafting a blog starts with researching before outlining, writing, optimizing for SEO, and editing. Here's how to carry out these processes using ChatGPT:

1. **Conduct research.** The first step to research is to find keywords to use in your blog post. All it takes is having a tentative topic for your blog post. You then ask ChatGPT to generate a list of keywords on your exploratory topic that are easier to rank for. It's a good idea to specify the number of keywords you'd like to have. You can ask ChatGPT further questions about the keywords it generates. Pick one keyword about which you'll write your blog post.

2. **Write an attention-grabbing blog post title.** Ask ChatGPT to write a certain number of blog post titles based on your chosen keyword. Ensure that you instruct ChatGPT to include your keyword in the title and the length of your title.

3. **Create your blog outline.** Ask ChatGPT to create an outline based on the topic you chose above. Ensure that your outline is unique so that you don't write a existing blog post. If you have other requirements, include them in your prompt.

4. **Create content.** Tell ChatGPT to write the content of a certain number of words and a given style for each subtopic in your outline. If you want the content to include facts and statistics, instruct it to include the sources used for cross-checking. You can also ask ChatGPT to rewrite certain portions of your content if necessary.

5. **Optimize your content for search engines.** The content produced above needs to be optimized for search engines if you want to attract or retain customers. With that in mind, ask ChatGPT to SEO-optimize your content based on your selected keywords.

6. **Edit and refine your content to sound like a person composed it.** While ChatGPT can edit text, it may be necessary to edit the content it produces so that it sounds like you wrote it.

How to Create Video Scripts With ChatGPT

Your content strategy isn't complete without video content because this format is popular. You can use video in ads, product descriptions, case studies, on-demand webinars, and many other types of content. Certain small businesses don't take advantage of video because they don't have the skills to write scripts and video production. ChatGPT can come in handy in video scripting, and here's an example of how to create a script for your YouTube video:

1. **Create your content, as we've explained, for writing a blog post.**
2. **Write your video script.** Instruct ChatGPT to turn the content above into a video script that runs for a specific time frame. If you want an animated video, specify so in your prompt. Add any other requirements you may have to produce an engaging video. ChatGPT will provide a script that includes illustrations you specify and voiceovers.

Your video script will not be perfect and require editing and modifying the illustrations. Even then, the process will be quicker than doing the whole task yourself. The above approach works for various video formats, such as webinars, online courses, newsletters, and case studies.

For a product description, you must provide the name of the product and its features and instructions, and ChatGPT will produce it.

Writing a Press Release With ChatGPT

Do you want to issue a press release, but you're unsure about how to do so or don't have much time? ChatGPT can quickly provide you with a press release to refine and issue it in time.

The process involves feeding ChatGPT with key points of your press release and context. For example, if you're launching a product, you could provide ChatGPT with the name of the product and its key features, when you're launching it, and its price during a given period of time. Remember to instruct ChatGPT to create the press release with little to no sales language.

How to Create Social Media Content With ChatGPT

ChatGPT isn't a great writing tool for long-form content, but it can be useful for short-form content like social media posts. Short-form content is helpful when you want to share condensed versions of your long-form content. For instance, you may want to tweet key points covered in your latest blog post.

The good news is that ChatGPT can pick up the difference between posts among various social media platforms. You can instruct ChatGPT to create a Twitter, LinkedIn, and Facebook post to promote one of your blogs. In your prompt, describe what ChatGPT should do and specify the platform on which you intend to use the post.

Feel free to experiment with different prompts until you get results that are close to what you desire.

How to Create Website Copy With ChatGPT

Your website is crucial because it links your business with its prospective customers. It should be SEO-optimized, persuasive, and engaging. A few years ago, you had to hire a copywriter to produce this content. Those days are gone due to the introduction of tools like ChatGPT.

The key elements of your website may include the various pages—home, about, sales pages, and products. Many websites also include the articles page, and you've learned how to write blog posts that appear on this page.

Let's illustrate how to create the home page with Chat-GPT. Suppose that your website focuses on selling a health supplement that supports healthy brain functioning. Before you feed ChatGPT with your prompt, you need to gather information such as product features and their benefits, your value proposition, your buyer persona, and at least three testimonials. It's crucial also to decide what action you want a visitor to take after reading your home page.

Now, treat ChatGPT as an expert copywriter versed in consumer psychology and brain functioning and knows how to drive website conversions. Begin your prompt by telling ChatGPT what role they will play to help you. Then, instruct ChatGPT to create your website's home page using your collected details—product features and benefits, buyer persona, value proposition, and testimonials. Inform ChatGPT to include a compelling headline, a persuasive introduction, and which keyword to SEO-optimize your page for.

How to Create Email Content With ChatGPT

ChatGPT can help you create various emails for lead generation, cart abandonment, product launches, follow-ups, and brand awareness. Effective business emails often follow similar patterns, making them ideal content to create with ChatGPT.

Suppose you want to write an email to your database of customers and test if there's demand for a product you want to introduce. An example prompt for ChatGPT could be:

"You're an e-commerce business that sells sports equipment. You want to introduce a new product, but you're unsure if your customers want it. Write an email that includes the [name of the product] and its features and benefits. Inform the recipient that the product is now available at a 40% discount in the next three days. Include a call to action (CTA). Include an attention-grabbing headline in your email."

If your customers are interested in the product, they'll buy it, which will indicate demand for it.

Of course, you can customize the above prompt with your type of business, product, or offer and even specify the Call to Action (CTA) you want. For your emails to be effective, it's worth creating a follow-up sequence to reach customers who don't see earlier ones.

The above prompt ideas can serve as bases for automating your content creation. We must emphasize the importance of fact-checking ChatGPT's content and checking that the brand tone and style are right for your business.

TIPS FOR CRAFTING EFFECTIVE CONTENT WITH CHATGPT

ChatGPT can save you time in your content creation process. One of the challenges with ChatGPT-created content is that it can lack the human touch and coherence and be less engaging. As stated earlier, ChatGPT doesn't have emotions, and readers can pick this up and not engage, leading to lower conversions.

There are ways to make the content generated by ChatGPT to be more engaging. It all begins with understanding your target audience. If you're unsure who your target reader is, how would you create content you know they'll read? You can't, and if you do, it'll be luck. Unfortunately, you can't maximize profits and efficiencies by relying on luck.

If you understand your target audience, you can include the tone, style, and sentiment in your prompts to personalize your content. Otherwise, you can conduct market research with ChatGPT to understand your target audience. All it takes is feeding ChatGPT with a market research prompt like this one:

"You're an expert market researcher in the finance industry. I want to create blog posts about credit cards and need first to understand my target audience. Give me the demographics and psychographics of people likely to read my articles in the US. Include their age, education, interests, income, likely locations, gender, financial challenges, and financial goals."

Remember to fact-check the facts and figures you receive for accuracy.

The next step you can take is to ask ChatGPT to provide you with topic ideas for the audience it has identified. You could ask it to include topic headlines for your content.

This way, you'll get personalized content ideas and headlines that grab the attention of your target audience. What's left is to select a topic and instruct ChatGPT to create your content, as discussed in the last section's prompts.

Remember that all the statistics and facts that ChatGPT provides should be double-checked for accuracy. ChatGPT can furnish you with outdated or incorrect information, and it's your duty to verify it. Some of the methods to verify ChatGPT facts and statistics include the following:

- Cross-check the facts against their original sources. This will be simpler if you ask ChatGPT to provide sources for the facts and statistics it shares.
- Consult two or three trustworthy sources such as market research reports, government publications, academic reports or articles, or news websites.

The major takeaway is that personalizing content with your target readers' interests will likely engage them. You can do this with ChatGPT by first understanding your audience.

COST-EFFECTIVENESS OF USING CHATGPT FOR CONTENT CREATION

There's a cost associated with content creation. The cost varies, depending on the format, length, and skill level of the writer. You have two approaches to getting your content written, which affect your costs: hiring a freelance writer or using your own in-house content creation team.

If you opt to have your own in-house team, you'll need at least a content strategist, content writers, and copywriters. The size of your team will depend on the amount of content you need. In the US, a content strategist earns around $94,700 annually, while a content writer or copywriter's salary is about $60,000 a year. An in-house team comprising these three professionals will cost you at least $214,700 ($94,000 + $60,000 + $60,000 = $214,000). These costs are a substantial content creation budget before we even consider adding graphic designers and video creators.

Alternatively, you could go for freelance content producers. A freelance content strategist may charge between $1,500 and $3,000 a month, depending on your project. Freelance writers vary based on content type and experience. You could be charged on a per-word or per-project basis. A 1,500-word blog article can cost $250 to $400 per project, though some writers can do the same for $1,500. A freelance copywriter may charge you from $1,500 to $3,500 for six pages of website copy (Lanier, 2023).

Another alternative is to hire a content marketing agency. Based on your scope and timeline, expect to pay anywhere from $2,500 to $10,000 per month.

Many small businesses don't have large enough budgets to pay the costs mentioned earlier. This problem is where

ChatGPT can be a welcome option. GPT-3.5 can save you between 60% and 90% for content creation and up to $200 per social media post. If a freelance writer charges you $400 per blog post, using GPT-3.5 can bring the cost down to $40 to $160. The more robust GPT-4 can shave from 30% to 50% in creating online tutorials while saving from 40% to 60% in the costs of video content creation. These substantial savings can help you scale your content and maximize revenues and profits more quickly.

It's worth keeping in mind that while ChatGPT can save content creation costs, you should use it responsibly and ethically. Also, keep in mind the quality of this tool's content and optimize it for engagement. More on legalities and ethics in a later chapter.

SAMPLE PROMPTS FOR STREAMLINED CONTENT CREATION

As you learned in Chapter 3, prompts are crucial for ChatGPT to provide the right kind of information or response you seek. Producing quality and engaging content with ChatGPT requires effective prompts. In this section, you'll find prompts for different types of content you can use as the basis for instructing ChatGPT.

Prompts for Creating Blog Posts

While you can first ask ChatGPT to create an outline for a blog, you can also directly request it to write an article.

You can also bypass the outline altogether and just ask ChatGPT to take the first crack at the article. The prompts below instruct ChatGPT to write draft blog posts within seconds or minutes, depending on length.

- "Create a [X]-word blog post about [topic]. Include the keyword [Y] in the headline as well as in all subtopics. Make the article informative and engaging, and target the interests and needs of readers of [topic]. Mainly use the active voice and write in a [tone] tone."

This prompt specifies the number of words you want and the topic. It also specifies the keyword the content should be SEO-optimized for. Use it when you've decided on the topic to write about and your target keyword.

- "Compose a blog post about [topic], including the benefits of the [topic], statistics, an engaging introduction, and a conclusion that mentions key takeaways. The blog post should be between [X] and [Y] words. Make sure the blog has no fluff, and you back up statistics you use with sources."

This prompt works well because it specifies the blog's topic and mentions key characteristics to include, such as the word count. Again, you'll use it when you've already determined your topic and know the number of words you want.

Prompts for Creating Engaging Video Scripts

Like all the others, these prompts should be clear for ChatGPT to write what you want. You need to provide enough information, such as the target audience and the purpose of your video. Here are prompts that can get you quickly started with the creation of YouTube video scripts:

- "Write a YouTube video script about [topic] to viewers who're looking to solve [problem]. Make the script seven minutes long, include fictitious example stories, real statistics, and provide five tips to solve [problem]. Present the script in a two-column table with the narration on the left and illustrations on the right."

People want to solve all kinds of problems, and this prompt can be used to help them do so in many industries or niches. Including a story will make the video relatable and engaging.

- "Compose a video script about a summary of the [book name]. The video should run for 10 minutes, include voiceovers and scene explanations, and have relatable examples to make the video engaging. Include how viewers can implement major lessons in the book in their lives."

This prompt is great for teaching readers certain skills that can improve their lives. You can use it to extract key points in any book that relate to your business.

Prompts for Writing Effective Newsletters

Newsletters perform various business functions, including building authority, generating leads, and converting leads into customers. You can also use newsletters to sell advertising space, especially if you have a large following. ChatGPT can help you create newsletters quickly by using prompts like the one below:

- "Create a newsletter that encourages [target audience] for a business that sells [product or service] to use it according to instructions. Show empathy, reinforce the importance of taking action, and reiterate the benefits of our [product/service]. The newsletter should be 700 words long and be helpful to our [target audience]."

The prompt works because it's clear about what ChatGPT should do. People buy products or services, and not many use them as they should or don't use them. This prompt aims to produce a newsletter to solve this problem.

- "Write a 600-word newsletter intended for [target audience] to educate them about [topic]. Be concise and specific, use the active voice and strong verbs, and minimize the use of adverbs and adjectives. End the engaging newsletter with a CTA to [desired action]."

This prompt is clear about what is required, making it work well. Use it when you want readers to take action, such as buying your product or subscribing to your newsletter.

The above prompts are for inspiration. Customize them to your business needs and see what content you get. Refine them if needed until you get quality content you can polish and make it match your brand's voice. As explained earlier, it's essential to cross-check statistics and facts to create up-to-date content.

ChatGPT does more than help with customer support and content creation. It can also come in handy for managing and improving your social media presence. The next chapter delves into this in more detail.

Hey there, fellow entrepreneur!

You're halfway through "Embracing ChatGPT for Business Success," and we'd love to hear your thoughts. Your feedback not only helps us but also fellow entrepreneurs seeking valuable insights. It's simple to leave a review on Amazon:

1. Visit the book's Amazon page by clicking the link or scanning the code below.
2. Scroll down to the 'Customer Reviews' section.
3. Click 'Write a customer review.'

https://www.amazon.com/review/create-review/?ie=UTF8&channel=glance-detail&asin=B0CML6QC6F

By sharing your experience, you're contributing to a community of entrepreneurs helping each other thrive. Let's make the entrepreneurial journey smoother for everyone. Your insights matter – thank you for being part of this journey!

5

SOCIAL MEDIA MARKETING REVOLUTION

"...I'm definitely going to start using it for some basic things. That, in combination with Canva, can be a game changer on social media."

— BLAKE SULLIVAN, MIDCON EXTERIORS

With ChatGPT, even a local shop can have a social media presence that rivals giant corporations. You can now effortlessly create a social media marketing strategy, posts or tweets, content calendars, and more without hiring a social media manager or agency. The costs you save can be reinvested in your business, thereby maximizing profits. All it takes is knowing how to use ChatGPT to accomplish these business-building tasks.

When you finish reading this chapter, you'll be able to perform these tasks quickly.

UNLEASHING CHATGPT IN SOCIAL MEDIA CAMPAIGNS

Social media is a powerful communication channel accessible to small and large businesses. It's an excellent tool for connecting with your customers, understanding your target audience better, and generating sales. You're missing out if you're not effectively using it or not on it. Here's why.

Nearly five billion people globally are on social media, constituting 93% of internet users (Newberry & McLachlan, 2023). Social media ranks within the top three channels that people aged 16 to 54 use to research brands before making buying decisions. This channel is still essential for the same purpose for age 55 to 64, as it appears in the top five channels used (Kemp, 2023). Based on this information, your target audience is likely on social media.

The crucial action is determining which social media platforms house most of your target audience. It's necessary to know this since you can't be on all social media platforms, or else you complicate your marketing efforts and reduce your efficiencies. Once you've figured out what social media platforms to use, you can enjoy the following benefits:

1. **Content promotion:** Social media opens opportunities to promote your content. In this way, your target audience can recognize your credibility and consider your business when making purchasing decisions. The good news is that you can promote various content, including text, images, and video. As such, you can improve the engagement of your target audience and potentially convert them into customers, increasing your revenues and profits.

2. **Better understanding of your audience:** Social media platforms offer audience insights that can help you know your audience better. This allows you to create content and products or services that resonate with them.

3. **Increased website traffic:** Adding links to your social media content can increase website traffic. This, in turn, augurs well for your SEO efforts, as search engines will recognize that your website offers value. With increased website traffic, you can maximize revenues and profits.

4. **Enhanced brand awareness:** Social media exposes your business to more potential customers and increases your brand's awareness. This increased visibility can lead to more generation of sales leads and enhanced revenues and profits.

5. **Increased engagement:** Social media platforms allow people to interact with your content. They

can share, like, or comment, allowing you to interact with potential customers. Because some social media platforms offer online reviews, you can also engage with your existing customers. This will enable you to promote your products or services and increase revenues.

When you consider that a person spends an average of 2.5 hours on social media daily, your brand can only benefit from this channel (Podium, 2022). What you need is to have a social media presence to reap the benefits mentioned above. It can be challenging for small businesses to do this well due to a lack of time and money. OpenAI's ChatGPT can come to your rescue and help you accomplish numerous social media tasks, including these:

1. **Creating a social media marketing strategy:** You need a strategy for your social media efforts to be effective. It can take a while and extensive effort to create this strategy. ChatGPT can help you do this, saving you time, effort, and money.

2. **Handling customer inquiries on social media at scale:** ChatGPT can instantly provide personalized responses to customer inquiries. ChatGPT can do this 24/7 and help multiple customers at once. This enhances your customer experiences and can help keep them longer and buying often.

3. **Creating social media posts:** ChatGPT helps you create engaging social media posts or X (previously Twitter) threads within seconds. The good news is that this tool can create posts suitable for different social media platforms. ChatGPT can also repurpose your longer-form content into social media posts, freeing time to handle more complex tasks.

4. **Generating social media captions:** ChatGPT can create personalized social media captions on applicable platforms like Instagram. These captions may increase the engagement of your posts.

5. **Crafting effective social media ad copy:** Running social media ads requires writing persuasive copy. You can do this with ChatGPT, eliminating the need to hire copywriters and saving labor costs for improved profits.

6. **Creating relevant images:** ChatGPT can provide image descriptions for creating social media images, though it can't make them alone. This saves you from having to find suitable pictures by trial and error. If you hire a graphic designer, you could hand them the image description, and they'll do the rest.

ENGAGING YOUR CUSTOMERS EFFECTIVELY

ChatGPT can be an invaluable tool to engage with your customers on social media platforms. Its power lets you answer customer questions, respond promptly, and initiate meaningful conversations.

To leverage ChatGPT, you need to monitor your brand's mentions, comments, and messages. Set up notifications so that you receive a real-time alert when a customer messages, mentions, or comments on your content. Of course, this assumes you will provide ChatGPT with a prompt to respond to a customer's inquiry, comment, or message. These responses can occur automatically if you integrate ChatGPT with a social media management tool.

Let's assume that you've not integrated ChatGPT with a social management tool, and you still want to leverage the power of ChatGPT. Here's how you can use ChatGPT to engage with your customers.

When someone mentions your brand's name, comments, or messages you on social media, you can ask ChatGPT to respond. Feed the customer's inquiry or message into ChatGPT and request it to personalize the response by mentioning the customer's name.

Once it does, review the answer and adjust it for brand voice before responding.

Adding emojis and other visuals can make your responses more appealing and engaging. While ChatGPT can't create images, it can suggest simple graphics to include in your response.

Remember that ChatGPT has no feelings and can't be empathetic. It may be helpful to read its responses to check if it sounds human or machine-like.

SAMPLE PROMPTS FOR SOCIAL MEDIA POSTS

There's a purpose behind posting social media content. Before you generate content with ChatGPT, it's essential to decide the purpose of the communication. This decision simplifies the crafting of ChatGPT prompts. Remember that every prompt needs to be specific and provide context to be effective. It's worth including the desired tone and style to elicit the emotions you want in your audience or followers. Here are prompts to get you started using ChatGPT to create engaging social media posts.

- "You have extensive experience as a [social media platform] marketer. Create a quiz about [topic/event] to encourage the [social media platform] community to engage with our brand—[business name].

A person can't just read a quiz because it requires the reader to interact with it. A well-designed and exciting quiz will likely be liked and shared with others.

- "Imagine you're adept at LinkedIn marketing and compose five posts to promote [product/service]. The tone and style of the posts should be [tone and style]. Our business's target audience's interests are [your target audience's interests], and their demographics are [demographics]. Include the buy call-to-action."

This prompt will get your audience to do something, making it easy to know whether your posts are compelling.

- "You're an experienced social media marketer. Craft a short-form video script about [topic] to use on TikTok, Facebook, YouTube, or Instagram. Make the video script intriguing and fun to elicit responses from our audience."

Curiosity is a critical element that makes people want to discover more. Therefore, it often leads to action. This call to action is what your social media posts should do, not just provide regular information.

The above prompts are starting points for leveraging ChatGPT and driving your business's revenues and profits. Consider modifying them to meet your specific needs or as foundations for other prompts. Most importantly, feel free to play with ChatGPT to create various types of social media posts. The more you do this, the more skilled you'll become in creating engaging social media posts with ChatGPT.

MEASURING THE IMPACT OF YOUR SOCIAL MEDIA EFFORTS

Measuring the performance of your social media marketing is the basis for ditching what doesn't work and keeping what works. When you discover what doesn't work, it's worth getting rid of it immediately. In contrast, when you find what works, you keep it. Doing what works and eliminating wasteful social media marketing activities will eventually maximize your return on investment (ROI) and your business's revenues.

Before you measure the impact of your social media activities, you need to identify relevant metrics. Fortunately, the social media marketing industry boasts standard metrics you can adopt. These metrics are divided into three main groups: social media engagement, social media marketing, and social media customer service metrics. A few also don't fall into either of these groups. Let's briefly explore strategic social media metrics to consider adopting and tracking.

Social Media Engagement Metrics

- **Impressions:** The number of times people on social media view your content can be measured at the content level or your profile level. An individual can have multiple impressions. Social media platforms measure this metric.

- **Engagement rate:** This is the total number of shares, reactions, and comments (called engagements) divided by your total audience size, multiplied by 100. For example, a social media profile with 2,000 posts and a piece of content that generates 12 total engagements has an engagement rate of 0.6% (12/2,000 x 100 = 0.6%). Whether this is good or not depends on your industry and your benchmark.

- **Audience or follower growth rate:** The number of new followers your business gains divided by your total audience over a given period. For instance, if your brand gets 20 new followers to increase the total to 2,500 during a certain month, your audience growth rate will be 0.8% (20/2,500 x 100 = 0.8%). Your audience growth rate is a function of how well you promote your business on social media.

- **Average amplification rate:** This refers to the ratio of the number of shares per post to your total audience expressed in percentage. For example, if the average number of shares per post is six and your total audience is 3,000, your average amplification rate is 0.2% (6/3,000 x 100 = 0.2%). The more your audience shares your content, the quicker the audience and brand grow, leading to increased sales leads and revenues.

- **Reach:** This means the number of people your content reaches. It can be measured per content or your business profile. A reach of 230 per post means that 230 people have seen your content since you posted it.
- **Virality rate:** This refers to the ratio of content shares to the total impressions and is expressed as a percentage. If a piece of content is shared 11 times and amassed 12,000 impressions, its virality rate will be 0.09% (11/12,000 x 100 = 0.9%).
- **Video views:** This is the number of people who watch your video. It doesn't necessarily tell you whether they've watched one second or the whole video. A video with 100 views has been seen by 100 people. Each platform determines what constitutes a view. For instance, watching a video on Facebook for the first three seconds counts as a view (Aguilhar, n.d.).
- **Video completion rate:** This is a fraction of total video views that run for the full course of a video. If a video has 350 views and 10 of them run until completion, then the video completion rate is 2.86% (10/350 x 100 = 2.86%). A high video

completion rate is a sign that your content resonates with your target audience.

Social Media Marketing Metrics

- **Click-through rate (CTR):** This refers to the percentage of impressions that result in clicking a link. A piece of content or an ad that contained a link that was clicked 20 times and had 15,000 impressions had a CTR of 0.13% (20/15,000 x 100 = 0.13%). CTRs vary by social media platform as well as industry. For instance, retail boasts an average CTR of 1.6% on Facebook ads (Barker, 2023).
- **Conversion rate:** This is the percentage of people who take the desired action after they are shown an offer. It's commonly used to measure the effectiveness of your copy. If 1,000 people click on a link that takes them to a landing page that offers a lead magnet, and 20 of them download it, the conversion rate is 2% (20/1,000 x 100 = 2%).
- **Cost-per-click (CPC):** This is how much it costs you for one person to click on your link on a social media ad. If you run a social media ad that gets ten links for a total cost of $200, your CPC will be $20 ($200/10 = $20). The lower the CPC is for a certain amount of sales, the more effective is your ad copy.

- **Cost per mile (CPM):** This is also called cost per thousand impressions, and it's the amount you pay to get 1,000 impressions. If you promote a piece of content on social media and it gets 20,000 impressions for a cost of $200, your CPM will be $10 (20,000/1,000 = 20 and $200/20 = $10).

Social Media Customer Service Metrics

- **Average response time:** This is the average time your customer support team takes to respond to a customer's inquiry on social media. Some social media platforms like Facebook show your audience your average response time. It's a good idea to make it as short as possible.
- **Customer satisfaction (CSAT) score:** This metric measures how thrilled customers are with your business, product, or service. You ask your customers to rate your business, product, or service on how happy they are with it. Then, you add all scores and divide by the number of survey responses, and multiply the result by 100 to arrive at your CSAT score.
- **Net promoter score (NPS):** This measures the loyalty of your customers to your business, product, or service. Calculating this metric starts with running a survey in which you ask,

"What's the likelihood you'll recommend our [business/product/service] to your colleagues, friends, or family members?"

Your customers respond with a score ranging from 0 to 10, with ten meaning very likely. Categorize each response into either the detractors (0–6), passives (7–8), or promoters (9–10) groups. Then, subtract the number of detractors from that of the detractors, divide the outcome by the number of responses, and multiply the answer by 100.

Other Key Metrics

- **Social share of voice (SSoV):** This refers to the mentions of your business on social media relative to the total number of your industry mentions. Calculating SSoV involves adding your brand's mentions across all social media networks and doing the same for your competitors. The sum of these mentions is the total mentions of interest. Divide the number of your mentions by the total number of mentions and express the outcome in percentage. This means that if the number of your mentions is 23 and those of your peers are 192, your SSoV will be 10.7% (23/(192 + 23) x 100) = 10.7%.
- **Social sentiment:** This measures the feelings and attitudes behind the mentions of your brand. If you want to figure out positive mentions, divide

positive mentions by the total mentions and express the result as a percentage. For example, if your brand has five positive mentions out of 110, the percentage of positive mentions is 4.5% (5/110 x 100 = 4.5%). You can perform a similar calculation for negative and neutral mentions. Tools such as Crowd Analyzer, Hootsuite Insights powered by Brandwatch, or Digimind can help you measure mentions.

ANALYZING SOCIAL MEDIA METRICS WITH CHATGPT

ChatGPT can help you evaluate the performance of your social media efforts. These evaluations allows you to use objective information to adjust your social media strategy to meet your goals. To analyze your performance metrics, ChatGPT requires your social media data. You can get this data from social media management tools like Hootsuite, Buffer, or Sprout Social or social media platforms.

Social media management tools allow you to schedule posts, track their performance, and collaborate with your team. Instead of logging into each social media platform's interface, you can manage your social media activities from a single tool. ChatGPT can access and analyze your social media performance data from these tools if integrated.

We will cover integrations more thoroughly in Chapter 8. Suppose you don't have a social media management tool. In that case, you'll need to manually feed your social media performance data directly into ChatGPT.

Whatever method you choose, you must first establish your goals for your social media campaigns. Determine whether you want to drive brand awareness, increase leads, or boost your sales. Knowing your goals allows you to monitor and analyze the relevant metrics.

When you have goals and have collected the social media data you need, it's time to take the next step. Download or export your social media platform's insights, and then copy and paste the data into ChatGPT and ask it a question such as:

"Can you analyze the sentiment in our previous five Facebook posts?"

The questions you ask will depend on what insights you want to have. Keep in mind that ChatGPT can provide an analysis report or trend of the performance of your social media efforts. You can also use it to analyze the social media performance of your competitors. Creating monthly and quarterly social media performance will be a breeze with ChatGPT.

Remember that your human judgment complements the analysis and insights that ChatGPT provides.

It's time to implement what you've learned about using ChatGPT for your social media efforts. Begin by asking it to provide you with a social media strategy tailored to your type of business. When done, request ChatGPT to create five posts per social media platform you want to use. Select the social media metrics you want to monitor on each platform. Once you have done all this, you'll have the foundations to continue with ChatGPT for social media success.

While social media is crucial for businesses, it doesn't provide deeper insights into customer behavior. You need in-depth data analysis to decipher your customers' behavior for improved engagements, revenues, and profits. This is where the next chapter will come to your help.

6

DATA ANALYTICS FOR SMARTER DECISIONS

"I was resistant to using ChatGPT for a long time and felt like using AI would be a betrayal to my own abilities and creativity. But when I finally gave in, I wished I had used it sooner because it saves me so much time on marketing."

— ANDREA BALL, ELEVATED WELLNESS

NWA

Small businesses collect all kinds of information, including marketing, sales, production, logistics, and IT data. When combined, this data is enormous and can be overwhelming to analyze. Unsurprisingly, businesses don't use between 60% and 73% of their data (Gualtieri,

2016). While 51% of small businesses believe it's crucial to collect data, only 41% of them gather it (Weston, 2022).

Not collecting and using your data can cost you thousands of dollars every month. For example, you may need opportunities to generate extra revenues or maximize profits. Luckily, ChatGPT can lift the heavy burden of analyzing vast amounts of data and help you gain a competitive edge. This chapter enables you to learn how to use this tool and take advantage of all the data your business gathers daily.

LEVERAGING CHATGPT FOR DATA COLLECTION

Before we dive into how to use ChatGPT, it's essential to learn why you need data and data analysis in your business. Data analysis will impact how you conduct customer support, run operations, solve problems, make business decisions, and other business activities. In turn, your business will begin to operate at a new level. Some of the reasons you should take data and data analysis more seriously include the following:

1. **You'll provide improved customer service.**
   Collecting data about the needs and wants of your customers helps you understand them better. For instance, if an analysis of your customers reveals that they need a particular product, you'll produce it cost-effectively. The reason is that you'll recoup

your production costs because your customers will buy it. In contrast, if your data shows that your customers don't purchase a particular product that much, you can stop producing it and save yourself money.

2. **You'll become better at identifying problems and solving them.** Analyzing data exposes issues that may be difficult to pinpoint with the naked eye. These hidden problems could be reasons for failure to hit your business goals. When identified, you can look for solutions and implement them. Whether those solutions are effective or not will again need further data analysis. If the research shows that the problem you had has disappeared, you can move your focus elsewhere. Otherwise, you'll need to revisit the issue and employ different solutions. You'll need to analyze your data to ensure your solution works.

3. **You'll improve your business's efficiencies.** Your data and its analysis simplify tracking the performance of your business against its milestones or objectives. If you're short on hitting your goals, you could investigate and rectify the causes behind the failure. Even when you meet those goals, data analysis can help optimize the efficiencies and streamline your business operations. These improved processes will spare you time to focus on more critical business areas and improve your chances of nailing your goals.

4. **Your business can improve revenues and profits.** Increased business efficiencies and a better understanding of your operations can lead to revenue increases. For example, if you employ your data to improve customer service, your existing customers may buy more often. The result will be increased revenues and profits because of lower customer acquisition costs. Data analysis helps you identify areas where you could optimize expenses and maximize profits.

5. **Your business will make better decisions.** As a business owner, you face many situations that demand quick decision-making. For instance, the naked eye may tell you your business has grown enough to move to its next growth stage. Your revenue may support your observations. The issue is that you can't base your scaling decision on revenue alone; you need an overall view of the business, which is where business data and its analysis will be useful.

6. **You can optimize the prices of your products or services.** Basing your prices on what competitors charge and what your research suggests may be a mistake. It's usually your customers who determine what prices to charge. An overall understanding of your customers using data you collected about them may signal that it's worth charging higher prices. The reason is that customers often buy products or services based

on the value they attach to them. If your data suggests your products or services are valuable to your customers, why not charge prices matching that value? You can as long as you analyze your data properly.

USING CHATGPT TO ANALYZE YOUR VALUABLE BUSINESS DATA

One of the primary reasons business owners give for not analyzing their companies' data is lack of time. ChatGPT helps solve this problem by analyzing massive amounts of data in minutes. You can use it to analyze data such as your website traffic, social media performance, customer surveys, customer demographics, and email marketing performance.

ChatGPT's free and paid versions can both help you with data analysis. With the free version, you need to enter a prompt and paste the data to be analyzed. The paid version does more than this: It allows you to upload data files such as CSV, plain text, Excel, and HTML and create various graphs. Irrespective of the version you use, your data analysis process is essentially the same. It works like this:

- **Step 1: Feed ChatGPT with the data you want it to analyze.** Ensure the data has headings, rows, and no empty fields within your data tables. If you're using the paid version, you can ask it to clean the data at this stage. If your data has customer personal data, first anonymize before you input it into ChatGPT to protect your customers' privacy.

- **Step 2: Enter your prompt to ask for data analysis, making sure to be specific and concise.** ChatGPT gives vague and generic responses if you don't tell it precisely what you want it to.
- **Step 3: Enter follow-up prompts until you receive a complete analysis of your data.** Again, be concise and specific.

Here are areas where ChatGPT can be helpful in data analytics and help your business make informed decisions:

- **Customer data analysis:** Many small businesses collect customer data such as names, email addresses, phone numbers, physical addresses, purchase histories, website browsing behaviors, and demographic information. ChatGPT can help you analyze this data to provide better customer service, sell more products or services, and create new products or services your customers want. For instance, Morgan Stanley uses ChatGPT to analyze the bank's historical data to help its financial advisors make better customer offers.

- **Sales and financial data analysis:** ChatGPT can analyze your financial statements and provide insights. You can analyze financial data that spans several years, identify trends, and figure out how to optimize revenues and expenses. ChatGPT can also spot trends in your financial data and help make more accurate forecasts. You can also identify areas where you need to invest more and maximize cash flows and your business's net worth. ChatGPT can also help you optimize your invoice payments by analyzing invoices and payments. It may analyze your payments and help you discover customers who almost always pay your invoices late. With this insight, you could find ways to replace this customer with a better one and maximize your revenues.

- **Customer reviews and feedback data analysis:** With ChatGPT, gone are the days of doubting to run extensive customer surveys and analyzing customer feedback data. All it takes is to organize and clean the data and feed it into ChatGPT, and you'll get insights into your customers. For instance, you'll discover what's most concerning about your products, services, and business. You'll also find out what new features or products they want. UberEats successfully conducted this kind of review to discover the ten common negative words used by their reviewers in the App Store.

This analysis led to an understanding of the customer sentiments toward this app.

REAL-WORLD EXAMPLES OF DATA-DRIVEN STRATEGIES

Analyzing massive amounts of data and having insights is only the start toward improved revenues and optimized profits. You also need to generate strategies to make those insights from the data and measure the impact on your business. Others have already demonstrated the system they implemented following data analysis. Here is a small sample of such methods and the companies involved:

- **Improving efficiencies in logistics:** United Parcel Service (UPS) is a leading logistics company globally that wanted to optimize its logistics operations. Of major concern to the company was delivering packages quicker, reducing errors, and optimizing its supply chain. It used AI-powered technologies to collect and analyze shipping times, shipping errors, and customer satisfaction rates. UPS implemented the insights gleaned from the data and reduced delivery errors by 75% while increasing customer satisfaction rates by 60% (Adrianne, 2023).
- **Increasing rankings on search engines:** HubSpot, a top marketing software provider, wanted to dominate SEO rankings by using

content. It needed to create and publish engaging, SEO-optimized content to achieve this objective. It used AI technology to analyze its industry keywords and competitors. This research resulted in crafting content plans based on data insights. Once it employed its content plans, it optimized its search engine visibility. This, in turn, boosted its website traffic and revenue (Aaltonen, 2023).

- **Optimizing content headlines:** The New York Times wanted to increase the readership of its content and keep those readers on its website longer. This required the headlines of their content to be more engaging. To create such headlines, the New York Times conducted A/B split tests on numerous headlines created by AI to determine the most impactful ones. Not only did this save time, but the data-driven headlines were more effective and led to increased reader involvement (Aaltonen, 2023).

- **Tailoring offerings to ideal customers:** American Express recently took advantage of the power of AI tools in driving its profits. It analyzed its massive volume of customer data and identified customer groups that drove its revenue growth. It used those insights to customize its offerings based on customer preferences, behaviors, and spending habits. The results of its efforts include increased customer engagement and retaining its leading position as a financial services provider (Adrianne, 2023).

To achieve similar results as the companies mentioned above, relying on AI-powered tools alone for data analysis and interpretation is insufficient. Still having professional analytics tools would be best, especially for analyzing complex datasets. For waterproof analysis, you also need to introduce the human element to make informed decisions.

GAINING A COMPETITIVE ADVANTAGE THROUGH ANALYTICS

Collecting data is the first step in improving business efficiencies and driving revenues and profits. Data you don't analyze is as good as not having it. Imagine that you've conducted a customer survey and received 250 responses. For some reason, you leave the data unused.

Unused data can't help you run your business better. That's why collecting data before you decide why you need it is not helpful. Ensure you conduct thoughtful surveys and use the data you collect. Once you have set your goal, your next step is to use it to analyze it to establish if you've reached your objective or not. In the case of the example survey mentioned above, an analysis may help you determine why you have high customer attrition rates. With that insight, you can formulate strategies to achieve your business goals.

Analyzing your business data should be empowering because ChatGPT can do this task quickly. All you do is provide the data to analyze and instruct ChatGPT on what to do. Later, we'll cover how to write effective prompts for data analysis. Even more critical is that Chat-GPT, as explained earlier, can provide insights from large volumes of data. This analysis can give you the edge against your competitors in the following ways:

- **It helps you understand your competitors.** If you dream of being the market leader in your industry, you need to know where you stand against your competitors. You need to compare your business with your peers in product or service offerings, marketing performance, logistics, and customer engagement. The insights will help you identify growth and improvement opportunities to stay competitive.
- **It assists with the improvement of business efficiencies.** Data analytics provides strategic information regarding the performance of your business. In the process, it exposes business inefficiencies, which enables you to fix the correct issues. In so doing, you improve process efficiencies and increase production while lowering business expenses.

- **It can help you retain valuable employees for longer.** Employee retention and engagement can give your business a competitive advantage. Data-driven recruitment makes it possible to analyze vast amounts of employees' work histories to detect potential long-term employment. The longer you retain experienced employees, the less money you'll spend on training. The main training cost will be associated with introducing new tools and technology. Your business will be more competitive because of lower recruitment costs and higher employee retention rates.

- **It helps you generate innovative ideas.** Analyzing competitors and your existing data helps identify areas where you can become more innovative. For instance, you may spot creative ideas that lead to new products, effective marketing campaigns, or improved customer engagement. This will differentiate you from competitors who fail to use unused data.

- **It assists with an in-depth understanding of your customers.** A thorough analysis of existing customer data can help you discover your customers' needs before they know it. With that insight, you can develop solutions that meet their needs before anyone does, which can give you a competitive edge.

- **It assists you to prepare for the future.** While no one can predict the future, trends can help you anticipate it. This is vital in today's world, where you need to adjust due to the ever-changing competitive landscape. Data analysis can reveal emerging trends and forecast what may happen. This will allow you to adapt your marketing, product development, customer support, logistics, and other critical business areas to stay relevant and be competitive.

We're living in fortunate times because AI tools and ChatGPT can help us analyze massive stacks of data. It's up to us to use that data to enjoy the benefits just mentioned above.

PROMPTS FOR DATA ANALYTICS

If you want to jump into data analysis with ChatGPT, this section is your hands-on guide. It's time to make sense of the data you've gathered over the past months or years. The tools for getting ChatGPT to provide insights on your data are prompts. For data analytics prompts, the key is to make them specific and concise, not forgetting to position ChatGPT as a data analytics expert. Here are examples of prompts to get you started on the right foot.

- "You're a top data analyst for a business in the clothing sector. Use the dataset provided to help us identify the correlation between customer satisfaction and sales revenue over the past five years."

- "As an expert data analyst, use your expertise to identify anomalies in the customer survey data provided. Suggest how to clean the data for accurate analysis."

- "You're wearing the hat of an expert data analyst. Our business wants to plan for the future and needs an accurate sales and profit forecast. Use the provided dataset to forecast our sales and profits in the next three years. Provide insights into how you arrived at your forecast."

- "As an experienced data analyst, we want you to help us spend our marketing budget on the right advertising platform. Analyze the dataset provided to determine which platforms delivered the best return on investment over the past five years."

- "You're a data analyst at our toys company that sells toys for kindergarten-aged children. From the dataset provided, figure out the profile of a parent to whom we should promote our toys."

- "We would like you to help us with your data analyst expertise to understand the sentiment about our company on social media platforms. Use the dataset provided to determine whether people view our company positively, neutral, or positively."

- "You're an expert data analyst who understands business finances. Our company wants to determine how best to optimize its cash flow. Analyze the cash flow statement provided and suggest how to make the best of our cash."

There are many data analytics prompts you can use depending on the dataset you have and your goals. A single prompt may only sometimes get ChatGPT to deliver your desired results. Or, you may want to know more from its analysis. In either case, you'll need to keep prompting until you receive the analysis and insights you desire.

Note that the above prompts may not necessarily apply to your business as they are. You'll need to customize them to your circumstances, and business needs for the best analysis and insights.

The business data you collect shouldn't go to waste as it can give you a competitive edge. It needs to be analyzed and insights derived for implementing data-driven strategies aimed at maximizing revenues and optimizing efficiencies. Business decisions based on gut feeling are rarely accurate and don't yield sustainable results. The same data-driven thinking should enter into what you do for lead generation and sales, a topic we delve into in the next chapter.

7

CHATGPT FOR SALES AND LEAD GENERATION

"Instead of writing perhaps 1-2 articles or blogs in a week, ChatGPT can help you write more than 6-8 in a week so it's truly beneficial. You will reach more audience = more opportunities and coverage."

— RIA RODRIQUEZ-RICHARDSON, MISS ENERGY, LADY BOSS

Think about this: How much would your revenue increase if you could qualify leads in real time? Whatever your answer is, it can happen without increasing the number of your sales personnel or hiring expensive copywriters. This means not only will you increase your revenues, but you can catapult your profits.

The way to achieve this is by properly using ChatGPT in real time. This chapter guides you on how to do this and includes lead generation and sales prompts to get you up and running quickly.

THE ROLE OF CHATGPT IN SALES PROCESSES

ChatGPT can be a powerful tool for streamlining and automating various stages of the sales process. To identify areas in sales where you could use ChatGPT, you need to understand your sales process. A typical sales process consists of the following steps:

- **Prospecting or lead generation:** This step involves finding new potential customers called sales leads.
- **Qualifying sales leads:** This is about determining if your leads are a good fit for your products or services. You need to interact with your sales leads to understand them better.
- **Researching your leads:** This step aims to understand the needs of your sales leads more deeply so that you can tailor your offer to them.
- **Making an offer:** This is also called pitching and presents the features and benefits of your product or service to qualified sales leads. It also includes pricing and other offer elements, such as guarantees.

- **Handling objections:** This step is aimed at allaying the fears of your qualified sales leads so that they can buy. Some of these would have been handled during the previous step, but sales leads may have additional questions that need to be answered.
- **Closing:** This is when a sale occurs or doesn't occur. If a sale occurs, you can move to the next step. Otherwise, you may need to discover other objections and handle them.
- **Nurturing and upselling:** This step is for retaining the customer for as long as possible.

With the understanding of the sales process, how can ChatGPT help you maximize your revenues and profits? Here are a couple of ways this tool can be helpful.

- **Performing repetitive sales tasks:** There are some tasks throughout the sales process that are repetitive. For instance, your business may generate sales leads using lead magnets and emails. ChatGPT can help you create as many lead magnets as you need, blog posts, white papers, case studies, video content, and emails to nurture your leads. During lead qualification, you could use surveys created with ChatGPT.
- **Objection handling:** Another sales process that can significantly benefit from ChatGPT is

objection handling. Prospective customers of your product or service often ask similar questions to determine purchase decisions. You can create FAQs and train ChatGPT to provide automated responses and real-time interactions.

- **Personalizing interactions:** ChatGPT can help smooth out the sales process by analyzing your customers' data. It achieves this by generating personalized responses based on past interactions and customer data. This can help you generate leads, qualify them, or close sales. What's astounding about ChatGPT, when used for lead generation, is that it can estimate the likelihood of a potential customer buying. It analyzes the language and sentiment the lead uses in interactions with it. It scores them for their probability of becoming a customer. If it deems a potential customer likely to buy, it could automatically close the sale with an email or link in the chat.

- **Nurturing sales leads:** Once you've generated qualified sales leads, they don't automatically buy in many instances. As many as 80% of your sales leads don't become customers. You'll need to nudge them to buy, so nurturing your sales leads becomes crucial. Properly nurturing your leads can help you convert 50% more of them to customers at a third of the cost (Saleh, 2023).

Some potent lead nurturing strategies include email marketing, social media marketing, sales calls, and content marketing. In each of these strategies, ChatGPT can play a crucial role.

- **Crafting sales presentations:** As we mentioned earlier, ChatGPT can be your copywriter. This is crucial for creating your sales presentation, whether in video or text format. In many cases, you'll use the same sales presentation repeatedly, especially if you operate an online business. You can create your primary sales presentation with ChatGPT and adjust it when needed.

- **Recommending other products or services:** ChatGPT can track your customers' behaviors and recommend additional products or services that complement their purchase. This strategy can help maximize sales per customer and your revenues.

Overall, ChatGPT can enhance customer experiences from when they start interacting with your business until they become your customers. Improved customer experiences can lead to repeat business and reduced customer acquisition costs. ChatGPT can also handle multiple customer interactions at the same time, which leads to increased revenues. When you combine this with labor cost savings and increased efficiencies, your business will become more profitable.

Businesses such as the B2B software company Pricefx and American Express India have used AI and ChatGPT-like chatbots to streamline and improve the efficiency of their sales processes.

Before Pricefx employed an AI chatbot, many people spent 22 seconds on its website before leaving without taking the desired actions. The marketing team added an AI chatbot to the website to gather visitor insights—who they were, the visitor source, and their location. With this information, Pricefx conversed seamlessly with its website visitors and engaged in personal conversations. The chatbot also suggested content the visitor could consume based on their interests. The company increased meeting bookings from its website by 17% while visitors' time on its website improved to one minute and 35 seconds (Burstein, 2023).

Not long ago, American Express India employed SMS campaigns to generate leads and customers. Its SMS campaigns were wildly successful, getting as much as 90% open rates. Eventually, its target customers stopped to respond to messages. The company decided to include a link to an AI chatbot, and its results improved by 49.3%. Buoyed by these results, American Express India intro-duced chatbots for car application reminders (Arasa, 2023).

While ChatGPT can help improve your sales results, bear in mind that success varies based on the type of business and your goals, industry, and chatbot quality and its implementation.

The Importance of Lead Qualification and Upselling in Increasing Business Revenue

By simply qualifying your sales leads or upselling your existing customers, you can boost your revenue. Lead qualification occurs once you have potential customers while upselling kicks in once a customer has bought at least one of your products or services. How do these two processes enhance your business revenue?

Successful prospecting brings all kinds of leads to your business. Not all of these are ready to become customers due to factors such as lack of money, lack of decision-making power, or they don't trust your business. If your business expends its efforts trying to convert these leads into customers, it'll be a waste of time, money, and energy.

The purpose of lead qualification is to identify people who are likely to buy your product or service. It would be best if you carried it out early in your sales process to avoid wasting business resources. Proper lead qualification aims to find leads who:

- are your ideal customer,
- are likely to need what you offer,
- can benefit from your products or services,
- have the authority and budget to purchase your products or services.

When your business spends its chunk of resources on qualified leads, it'll be more efficient and make more sales per given period; more sales translate to higher revenue. With that said, don't throw away disqualified leads. Keep nurturing them for possibly converting them into customers in the future.

Upselling is selling your existing customers more of your products or services. The great thing is that your ROI for such sales will be higher because your customer acquisition cost is zero. It can cost you six to seven times more to acquire a new customer than to retain one (Bernazzani, 2022). Retaining customers is therefore crucial not only for shooting up your revenue but also for optimizing profits.

To illustrate the impact of upselling, suppose that your business generates $100,000 per year in revenue and has 5,000 customers. On average, each customer contributes $20 to the revenue. After realizing the benefits of upselling, you offer your existing customers another product related to what they've purchased in the past. Suppose a quarter of your customers buy a new product that costs $25 each per year. In that case, your revenue will increase by $31,250 annually—that's a 31.25% annual revenue increase.

The good news is that you can upsell your customers irrespective of your industry or type of business. If you don't have an additional product or service to sell, consider creating it. Otherwise, you can find an affiliate product or service that complements your offer and sell it to your customers.

How to Program ChatGPT to Identify Promising Sales Leads and Upsell Opportunities

Nothing frustrates someone like trying to sell a product or service to a stranger. Because the person doesn't know you or trust your business, it'll be hard to get them to separate from their dollars. In contrast, it's easier to sell to someone who has shown some interest in what you offer. It's even easier if you sell to someone immediately after they've demonstrated that interest, which is where ChatGPT comes in.

For this to happen, you should have integrated ChatGPT into your lead generation and sales systems. More details about ChatGPT integration into your business systems are covered in Chapter 8. To program ChatGPT to take advantage of promising sales leads and upselling opportunities, you should train your ChatGPT with your lead generation and sales materials.

The minimum to consider doing for this purpose is integrating your ChatGPT with your customer relationship management (CRM) tool, website, and social media platforms. This will allow you to automate lead capturing and move your leads through your sales funnel until they buy.

ChatGPT will spot upsell opportunities for existing customers and help you maximize sales and profits.

PROMPTS FOR SALES AND LEAD GENERATION

This section will be your practical guide if you'd like to leverage ChatGPT for business lead generation and sales. You'll discover examples of prompts you can use for both inbound and outbound lead generation and sales. Understand that how you approach potential customers will differ based on how you meet them.

Both inbound and outbound processes for generating leads and closing them include the awareness, interest, decision, action, and retention stages of your sales funnel. Here's a quick reminder about what each is accomplishing:

- **Awareness:** This stage kicks in when you interact with the potential customer for the first time. Assets like social media posts, ads, lead magnets, cold calling, or cold emailing or calling could connect your business with possible customers.
- **Interest:** Potential customers who show interest in your product, service, or business get qualified.
- **Decision:** This is the stage when you provide qualified leads with information to make purchase decisions. Handling of objections falls in this stage.

- **Action:** This is the stage for converting qualified leads into customers. Your job is to make an offer your leads will find hard to resist. The ability to create persuasive sales material is crucial.
- **Retention:** This is when you keep in touch with your customers to keep them engaged and to best use your products or services. It's also a good time to sell more products or services to your existing customers.

With that out of the way, let's review example prompts you could use for lead generation and sales.

- "You're the owner of a successful [industry] company based in [state and city]. You want to generate leads cost-effectively. Create a friendly [number of words]-word LinkedIn post about [topic] that adds value to [target audience]. Focus it on [keyword] and include this keyword [number of times]."

This prompt is ideal for inbound lead generation at the awareness stage when you want to showcase your industry authority. It's a good approach when you want to indirectly demonstrate you can solve your target customer's pain points or help them achieve their goals.

- "You're an expert email marketer, and you want to reach out to potential customers in [industry].

Craft a personalized cold email in a friendly tone that is empathetic to your target audience's pain points and informs them about your solutions. Include methods to follow up the leads to convert them into customers."

This prompt works well for generating leads with cold emails.

- "Suppose that you're a copywriter and you want to qualify leads for [business name] in the [type of industry] industry. Write ten possible questions to qualify your potential customers."

This prompt is for potential customers who have shown interest in your product, service, business, or competitors. It aims to determine if a lead could be moved to the next stage of the sales funnel.

- "We operate a [industry or niche] business, and we want to help our qualified leads to make purchase decisions. Give us five topics that we can write about to overcome objections our leads may have to buy our [product or service name]. Also, suggest captivating email headlines that will increase the open rates of our emails to these leads. Include call-to-action descriptions that entice our leads into taking the desired action."

This prompt aims to obliterate objections and convert leads into customers. Notice that the prompt is specific to get ChatGPT to do what's required.

- "You're an expert email newsletter marketer. Create six topics for each of the five email newsletters our [industry or niche] business can use to retain customers who bought [product or service]. Select practical topics that help our customers use our [product or service] effectively and get their desired results. Encourage customers to provide feedback in each of the newsletters."

With this prompt, you aim to retain customers by providing value. Your customer feedback could be used to improve your product or service or create a new product or service.

Remember to customize the prompts above for your business needs, customer base, and your brand voice, style, and tone. Refine them to get the kind of responses you want. Most importantly, use the above prompts as a basis for more lead generation and sales.

ChatGPT can improve your lead generation and sales efforts in multiple ways. You can train it on your sales information, such as product descriptions, FAQs, customer data, and other sales-related documents, to identify leads you can quickly convert into customers.

You can also spot customers you can upsell to maximize your revenues and profits. There's more that ChatGPT can do besides streamlining your sales process; it can improve efficiencies in many of your activities when integrated into your existing business systems.

8

INTEGRATING CHATGPT INTO EXISTING BUSINESS SYSTEMS

"I consider ChatGPT a great collaboration partner, but not some kind of genie that grants wishes."

— DUSTIN DOUGLAS, 3D TECHNOLOGY CONSULTANTS

"The best way to predict the future is to create it," said the renowned management consultant Peter Drucker (BrainyQuote, n.d.). Your business's future could be bright if you integrate ChatGPT into your current business systems, such as customer support, lead generation and sales, logistics, and other crucial functions.

For your ChatGPT integration to be effective, you need to follow a proven process, which you'll learn about in this chapter. Since no technology works perfectly all the time, we'll also cover how to fix issues when they arise.

STEPS TO INTEGRATE CHATGPT INTO YOUR BUSINESS OPERATIONS

Integration of ChatGPT into your business is no longer a luxury to enjoy by the few. Any business can integrate ChatGPT into its systems, maximize revenues, and improve efficiencies. It's crucial to properly integrate ChatGPT into your existing business systems to gain the most from it. There are multiple ways of integrating ChatGPT into your business. Your choice will depend on your goals and budget and will also guide your integration process.

You need to follow a step-by-step process to integrate ChatGPT into your business properly. It's crucial to get these steps right to save costs, time, and frustrations. Here are the steps:

Step 1: Identify Business Systems to Integrate With ChatGPT

The first step is determining the business systems that could benefit from ChatGPT integration. It's easy to think that every business system needs ChatGPT integration. Still, the task could be too big for many small businesses and entrepreneurs.

Discovering existing systems to integrate with ChatGPT starts with analyzing your current business processes. The processes to analyze include product development, marketing, sales, customer service, accounting and financial analysis, and logistics. The methods to consider integrating with ChatGPT tend to be more repetitive and time-consuming tasks, such as content creation.

Break down your business functions into tasks and evaluate how ChatGPT can add value to each task. You don't have to automate each task fully; some jobs may benefit from semi-automation.

Collaborating with your employees from different business areas is essential to find business activities to integrate with ChatGPT. These insights will ensure you get the buy-in from employees affected by the integration.

As we mentioned in Chapter 1, it's worth starting small when introducing AI and ChatGPT. That's why you need to prioritize the systems to integrate with ChatGPT. Trying to take on too much in a short space of time may lead to multiple failed integrations. Perhaps consider integrating systems that will provide quick wins; that may be the best route to choose.

Step 2: Set Goals for Integrating ChatGPT

The way to know whether your integration is a success or not is to measure its impact. That in itself doesn't tell you much unless you have a benchmark against which to evaluate the performance. The next step is to set benchmarks against which you'll measure the success or lack thereof of your ChatGPT integration.

One of the effective goal-setting frameworks requires that every goal you set be specific, measurable, achievable, relevant, and time-based, often represented by the acronym SMART. For example, if you decide to integrate ChatGPT into your customer service systems, one of your goals may be to "Increase customer satisfaction by 25% in the next 12 months." Avoid setting too ambitious goals because you'll increase your chances for failure. On the other hand, make your goals challenging so that you, your employees, and the business grow significantly.

Step 3: Select Your Integration Method

There are multiple ways of integrating ChatGPT into your business systems: using existing ChatGPT solutions, custom models, or repurposed products. Making the appropriate choice depends on factors such as your needs, goals, and your kind of existing systems.

- **Existing ChatGPT solutions:** These are pre-packaged AI tools, such as plugins for ChatGPT, that you can integrate with little technical expertise.
- **Custom solutions:** This is where you develop custom AI models tailored to your needs and are trained with your own business data. You need a

lot more resources, such as software developers and data science expertise, to properly execute this kind of integration. You can expect to pay a lot more than the above solution. The major pro of this approach is that it can give exclusive benefits, giving you a competitive advantage. There's a high level of scalability and flexibility that can come in handy as your business's needs change.

- **Repurposed ChatGPT models:** This is where you adapt ready-made AI products to fit your needs and goals. Approaching your ChatGPT integration this way may be cheaper and quicker to deploy. However, it would help if you still had software development and data science skills. You could face scalability challenges later due to the limited flexibility of the integration.

Before deciding on what integration method to choose, ask yourself questions like:

- What's our budget for ChatGPT integration?
- What are our ChatGPT integration needs and goals?
- What kind of systems do we want to integrate ChatGPT with?

Step 4: Develop Your Integration

This step is relevant if you opt for custom or repurposed ChatGPT integration solutions. Before you develop your integration, you need to hire the right expertise. You can hire freelancers or software development companies. Irrespective of the resource you're hiring, consider the following:

Find potential software developers through research, online and offline. It would be great if you could get referrals from your network. You don't want to be the first client of a software developer when so much is at stake. It's crucial to hire proven expertise in the area of interest.

Evaluate potential candidates to determine their fit with your needs. Check potential candidates' portfolios to confirm that they have ChatGPT integration expertise. If a candidate doesn't have such experience and knowledge, give them a pass.

When you've identified potential hires, compare their pricing and project timelines. Keep in mind that a software developer or data scientist may have the experience and expertise you require at a reasonable price and still be unreliable. Check with their past clients to gauge the attitude of each hire you're considering. If you're happy with a candidate, conduct interviews before hiring them.

Some places you could locate software developers and data scientists include Guru.com, Upwork, Turing, Fiverr, and Arc. Remember to search on your favorite search engine for potential candidates.

Once you have hired the required personnel, it's time to get them to develop your integration. To ensure smooth progress, it's worth monitoring the project. If you don't have the time to do this yourself, hire a project manager who updates you regularly about progress.

Step 5: Test Your Prototype

It's rare to integrate ChatGPT into a business system and find it fully responds positively the first time. You can't have a ready product until you have repeatedly tested and re-tested your solutions. Manufacturers do this to ensure that their products work as intended. For instance, a car must be tested to ensure it can reach the speed the manufacturer claims on its odometer.

After you've developed your ChatGPT integration, it's time to test-run it to ensure it works as desired. The test should imitate actual operating conditions as closely as possible. When you discover issues, fix them and run the test again. Iterate this process over and over until you have a product that's ready for deployment. When the prototype is good enough for your purpose, move to the next step.

Step 6: Train Your Employees

ChatGPT and generative AI technology are new, and many of your employees will need to be trained for maximum company benefit. Training your employees should be part of the integration project so that you can benefit from the expertise of software developers and data scientists.

The first crucial step to ensure proper training is developing engaging training materials. Your training materials should:

- Define objectives for your ChatGPT integration training.
- What the business hopes to achieve with the integration.
- Step-by-step instructions, including graphics, on how to use the ChatGPT integration.
- Provide practical exercises to help employees understand how to use the integration in theory and practice.

During training, make it clear that your intention with ChatGPT is to improve processes and efficiencies, not to get rid of their jobs. Emphasize that you want them to experiment with the integration to get the best out of it. Most importantly, demonstrate to employees how the ChatGPT integration will simplify their jobs and free them to focus on more complex and rewarding tasks.

Remember to have other support resources, such as FAQs and forums, to help employees during the transition to ChatGPT integration.

Step 7: Implement, Monitor, and Evaluate the Integration

Now that your product is good enough for your needs, deploy it. Before deployment, ensure you've taken steps to protect the privacy of your users. Also, ensure you use your ChatGPT solution legally and ethically to avoid potential lawsuits. Chapter 9 will delve into these issues and how to protect yourself.

Implementing ChatGPT doesn't mean you're set for life. You need to monitor its impact on your customers and employees and its performance against your goals. One of the ways to establish your solution's impact is to seek customer and employee feedback using tools like surveys. If it doesn't deliver the expected results, find out why and how to improve it. On the other hand, if the integration provides the desired results, consider integrating ChatGPT into another business system.

TROUBLESHOOTING ISSUES

Your use of ChatGPT may proceed flawlessly, and you may still encounter issues such as compatibility with your existing business systems. Reasons for this vary and may include the following:

- **Configuration errors:** These issues may occur due to software development during the integration process. If you've successfully tested your integration and it worked, the cause of the issues could be the latest updates to ChatGPT. Considering that ChatGPT is still new, we can expect more updates to come in the future. If your ChatGPT integration isn't set up to handle future updates, you could face issues with the technology. This is where having a custom ChatGPT integration may trump using the off-the-shelf version. You can solve this problem by getting an experienced ChatGPT developer to investigate and address the concern.

- **Connectivity troubles:** ChatGPT is a website-based technology that requires an internet connection to perform correctly. If your users' internet connections are sluggish, they may have difficulty engaging with your ChatGPT model. Sometimes, the connectivity troubles could be due to server maintenance issues. There isn't much you can do about this issue except inform your users to check their internet connectivity. Otherwise, ask them to try the system again later.

- **ChatGPT body stream error:** This error occurs when ChatGPT fails to generate a response to a user's request. This can prevent interaction with your integration with ChatGPT and result in a bad user experience. Causes for this error include API connectivity issues, code errors, the ChatGPT server being down, or missing data. To check the ChatGPT server's running status, head over to https://status.openai.com/. You'll also find the status of OpenAI's API and a history of the issues reported. Typically, OpenAI will resolve these issues within a few minutes.

If you've looked at all external issues that may hinder the proper functioning of your integration, it's time to look internally. This action may involve consulting a software developer or data scientist to check your integration. If this happens to be the case, get the first software developer to investigate the issue before consulting with another professional. While looking for solutions, let your customers know that you're experiencing issues with your integration and are working on finding a solution.

Ultimately, successfully integrating ChatGPT systems will depend on how well you follow the steps described earlier. When done well, your business efficiencies will improve, as will your revenues and profits. It'll also be easier to automate some of your business activities and free more of your time to focus on human-intensive tasks. Remember that the power you gain by integrating ChatGPT into your business systems comes with responsibility. For example, you need to adhere to various laws and regulations as well as ethical uses of ChatGPT—a discussion we will tackle in the next chapter.

9

LEGAL AND ETHICAL ASPECTS

"As someone with an academic background, the issue of plagiarism is real.

But as with other new advances, our society needs to teach practices to enhance critical thinking instead of ignoring new technologies."

— DR. BRYAN RAYA, DBR BOOKKEEPING,

DOING BUSINESS RIGHT

W hen it comes to AI, ignorance of the law and ethics is a risk you can't afford. Others have already found out the hard way that implementing AI and ChatGPT comes with some risks. It's incumbent on every business owner or entrepreneur to make sure that they use ChatGPT responsibly to avoid being raked across the coals. All this begins with understanding ChatGPT's legal landscape and ethical applications. This chapter delves into this and more to help you stay on the right side of the law.

NAVIGATING THE LEGAL LANDSCAPE OF CHATGPT USE

As you adopt AI tools such as ChatGPT, you can't turn a blind eye to legal frameworks aimed at ensuring you use the tool legally and ethically. There are key laws and regulations in the AI and ChatGPT world you should be familiar with, including these:

Copyright Infringement

OpenAI used vast amounts of online text-based information such as books, reports, blog posts, forum materials, and news articles to train ChatGPT. There's no guarantee that the ChatGPT output you get is free of copyright infringement. If someone claims you've infringed on their copyright, they could hold you legally liable. A case in point is Stability AI, which Getty Images claims used its copyrighted database to train its AI (Hines, 2023).

The U.S. Federal Trade Commission (FTC) and the EU are doing something about this challenge. The EU is creating regulations that will require revealing the sources of information used for AI training.

Another possible source of copyright infringements pertains to ownership of ChatGPT's outputs. It's unclear whether the responses you get from ChatGPT belong to you or its creator. OpenAI allows you to publish ChatG-PT's outputs, provided the publisher permits you to do so. The problem is that you can't be sure that ChatGPT's outputs are unique, which opens up the possibility of infringing on someone's copyright. That's why it may be unwise to use prompts without customizing them to your unique situation. It's even better to use ChatGPT for inspiration and avoid using its outputs verbatim.

Legal Documents and Notifications

There's no getting around the need to create legal documents such as letters of demand. The problem is that small businesses often lack the expertise and financial resources to develop such documents and notices. It can be tempting to resort to ChatGPT; after all, many people see this tool as a means to save costs and improve efficiencies.

ChatGPT can help you write legal information and documents such as contracts, warning notifications, and public notices. Its legal outputs appear sound from your point of view. Can your perspective and interpretation of the law be the same as that of an attorney if you're not a legal expert? An attorney may discover that your legal document is based on an outdated law or doesn't comply with the requirements of your city or state. It's a good idea to rope an attorney versed in the legal discipline of interest to comply.

Data Privacy and Regulation

ChatGPT training information may raise data privacy and regulation concerns. When you converse with ChatGPT, it generally stores your inputs and outputs. It then uses this information for training to make future models better. Users could include sensitive information such as an employee's income and personal details in their prompts that ChatGPT may add to its future outputs.

Sharing personal or sensitive information may violate data privacy laws and land your business in legal hot water. It's vital to inform users transparently to avoid inputting sensitive information in ChatGPT's conversation interface and explain why. Preferably, let users know they can instruct OpenAI to delete their content or manually disable ChatGPT's chat records.

Two popular data regulation policies to ensure you comply with are the CCPA and GDPR. As explained in Chapter 1, the CCPA protects California citizens' privacy rights, while the GDPR does the same for EU residents. Ensure you adhere to these regulations' requirements to avoid legal implications. Always let your users know that you're using ChatGPT in consumer interactions when you do so.

Trademark Violations

One area of concern when using ChatGPT is the possibility of violating trademarks. This is possible when you use this tool to generate business brand assets such as logos or company slogans.

If you use ChatGPT to create such brand identity assets, it's worth verifying that they're not trademarked. The easiest way is by consulting with a trademark attorney who understands the nuances of the trademark clearance process. If this attorney discovers that the assets you want to use are trademarked, you can seek permission from their owner or create new ones.

Generation of Biased or Inaccurate Information

The dataset on which ChatGPT is trained can expose you to copyright infringements, and it can also include inaccurate or biased information. For instance, it could occasionally generate discriminatory or offensive outputs. Because this tool can't self-introspect, it might not detect problems like these and eliminate them. This can expose you to legal action.

This concept might sound like theory when you consider the impact that ChatGPT is having in the entrepreneurship world. It's not, and a case in point occurred in April 2023. An Australian mayor sued OpenAI, claiming that ChatGPT inaccurately claimed that the police arrested and charged him for bribery in 2012. This kind of information can have reputational damage to your clients, customers, or users, leading to legal charges against your business.

Your troubles might not stop there, as you may lose business deals for presenting inaccurate information. For example, you might generate important information with ChatGPT to land a business contract. The information you supplied may have included material errors that can lead to legal nightmares.

Inaccurate information can also haunt your business if you dish out advice or how-to content. The online information that ChatGPT was trained on may include wrong or misleading information. It's your duty to ensure that the advice or how-to information you provide is sound and safe.

It's absolutely necessary to get a competent person to verify the accuracy of your information when you engage with clients or customers. Get this individual or vendor to provide sources where there's critical information.

ETHICAL CONSIDERATIONS

ChatGPT doesn't only present possible legal issues for business, but it also brings ethics challenges. No business can expect customers to stay with it if it breaks their moral standards. This makes it necessary to consider the ethical aspect of ChatGPT implementation in your enterprise. Some of the ethical issues you'll need to think about include the following:

Job Displacement

Automation with ChatGPT has irked some people because it threatens job security. While employment in the U.S. keeps increasing, unemployment hit 3.8% in August 2023. This percentage means about 6.4 million Americans are without jobs (U.S. Bureau of Labor Statistics, 2023). ChatGPT's capability to automate routine tasks raises concerns to ponder about and minimize its impact.

These concerns are unwarranted. As far back as 2013, researchers had incorrectly warned that computerization would eliminate routine-intensive jobs (Frey & Osborne, 2013). We know today that automation has changed the way businesses conduct their bookkeeping and accounting, inventory management, and logistics functions without the mass elimination of jobs.

ChatGPT is already disrupting jobs such as data analysis, computer programming, copywriting, and many media jobs such as content creation and copywriting. The good news is that humans aren't wired to perform the same position for the rest of their lives; they can train to perform new functions. Companies need to recognize this and train at-risk employees on new jobs. Most importantly, businesses need to emphasize that ChatGPT technology's main job is to help employees perform their jobs better.

Plagiarism and Cheating

Plagiarism is the act of passing off someone else's work as your own. Engaging in plagiarism is an act of theft—literary theft. You're taking someone's work as your own and potentially making money from it. Whether you're a content creator, legal assistant, marketer, or salesperson, using someone's content as your own is unacceptable. It's like someone scoring a touchdown, and you come in and claim it's you—it's unethical behavior.

Whether you plagiarize someone's content deliberately or by accident, it's still unacceptable—it's cheating. Plagiarism and cheating in content creation and academic circles have been concerns for decades. This matter has assumed a new level in the age of AI and ChatGPT. Part of the reason is that it can be difficult to detect plagiarism in ChatGPT-generated content.

The introduction of ChatGPT presents a quick method of creating large amounts of content. Content creators see this as an opportunity to make a quick buck or to finish their jobs quickly. There's nothing wrong with this thinking except that you claim the benefits that should accrue to someone else.

The first level of defense against ChatGPT plagiarism is to train your employees on the proper use of the tool. In the training, explain why plagiarism is ethically bad. Perhaps give them an outrageous example of stealing one of Shakespeare's works, such as Julius Caesar, and claiming it as your own. There's no way doing this will endear such a person with their audience.

Once you've trained your employees about plagiarism and the ethical use of ChatGPT, encourage them to provide sources for the facts and statistics it provides. These behaviors will ensure that your business doesn't claim someone's work as your own and keep it in its customers' good books. Also, encourage your employees to use proven plagiarism detectors before submitting content.

Biased and Inaccurate Outputs

We've already discussed that ChatGPT can churn out biases and inaccurate outputs. Not only can this lead to legal troubles, but it has ethical issues connected with it. One of the legal issues we referenced is the story of an Australian mayor who opened a defamation case against OpenAI due to ChatGPT outputting damaging and inaccurate information about them. Imagine what damage may be caused if ChatGPT outputs racial or stereotyped content!

We can't emphasize enough the importance of making your employees or ChatGPT users aware of this tool's limitations. Best of all, you can prevent these biases when training your ChatGPT model.

You can achieve this in two ways: avoiding representation bias and concept bias. Representation bias is the product of excluding certain groups of people from your training data, for instance, using training data that treats men or women as inferior to the other group. Trained with this bias, ChatGPT will generate content that favors one gender over the other.

Concept bias occurs when you train your ChatGPT based on ideas associated with a given set of people. For instance, if you train it with content that associates a particular group of people with traffic violations, it'll likely associate those people with that type of infraction.

It's crucial to clean your training data from biases such as gender, stereotypes, and discrimination. Not doing this may repel certain people from buying from your business, which would likely spell trouble for your business.

Privacy Violations

As mentioned earlier, ChatGPT and related AI tools are trained on vast amounts of online data. Unfortunately, some people's sensitive information may form part of this training data. When you request ChatGPT to assist you with some work, it may return someone's personal information.

Another possibility is that a user may input their or someone else's personal information in ChatGPT or your ChatGPT chatbot. This information will be used as training data if the user hasn't instructed OpenAI not to use their information for training purposes. As such, ChatGPT may later output that information depending on the prompt it received. You can't know what the recipient of such information will do with it. Not only does access to someone's sensitive information violate data privacy laws, it's also unethical. They may steal that person's identity, conduct phishing attacks, or impersonate that individual.

When you use AI tools and ChatGPT, inform users that you do so. Warn them to refrain from inputting their personal information in your AI tools to protect their identity and privacy. Also, advise them to request OpenAI to remove their historical ChatGPT conversations.

Copyright Infringement

OpenAI trained ChatGPT with a variety of online information. Some of those works may have been copyright-protected. When you prompt ChatGPT for a response, it could provide copyrighted content.

We asked ChatGPT this question,

"Do you provide sources when you use someone's content in your outputs?"

Here's its response, which you can regenerate by using our prompt:

"I don't use content from specific sources, websites, or databases in my responses. Instead, I generate responses based on a mixture of licensed data, data created by human trainers, and publicly available data. I do not have access to proprietary, classified, confidential, or subscription-based information.

If you have a specific question or need information on a particular topic, feel free to ask, and I'll do my best to provide a helpful response. If you're looking for sources or references, I can suggest general types of sources where you might find relevant information, but I won't be able to provide specific citations. It's always a good practice to verify information from multiple reputable sources when conducting research or seeking accurate information."

The problem is that publicly available data may be copyrighted, and you might end up with this kind of information. Note also that ChatGPT says it doesn't give specific sources. Yes, you wouldn't have deliberately stolen such content, but you'd have received content obtained unethically and illegally.

It's crucial that you double-check the content you get from ChatGPT for copyright infringement. This is especially true if the content contains unfamiliar words. Another action you could take is to develop an AI ethics guideline that directs your company on how you use AI and ChatGPT. Most importantly, inform your users that you're using a chatbot if they're conversing with your AI tool. Make it clear that inputting personal information may compromise their privacy. If you collect personal information, ensure that you get user consent before doing so. Other actions you could take to promote the ethical use of AI tools and ChatGPT are:

- Never publish any content, whether ChatGPT produced or not, that could hurt someone else. You can practice this by reviewing and refining your content through ChatGPT.
- Fact-check the accuracy of the facts and statistics that ChatGPT provides.
- Release every content provided you are certain what it says is true. Although verifying that you publish accurate content takes time, consider that doing otherwise may hurt someone. If you're unsure about the truth of what you say, add a source.
- Understand that your business promises its target audience something. If what you promise isn't genuine, you might hurt the success of your brand. Delivering what you promise is the trademark for trustworthiness.

It makes business sense to comply with all AI and Chat-GPT-related laws. A good test for whether you're complying is to ask, "How would I feel if my rights were violated?" Your rights include data privacy, copyright protection, and the right to be respected. Every person you interact with deserves the same level of respect and protection. Your primary aim when using AI tools and ChatGPT should be to enhance someone's life, not destroy it. In light of this, ensure that you respect the law and ethics.

While it's crucial to stay within the bounds of law and ethics, it's equally essential to ensure you enhance the performance of ChatGPT in your business. This involves understanding why it's not delivering the results you expect and fixing the issues you identify. The next chapter delves into this part of the ChatGPT application in detail for you to optimize your revenues and profits.

10

ENSURING LONG-TERM SUCCESS

"A.I. will not take over the world. The people that harness the power of A.I. will."

— ADAM ROBISON, NORTHWEST
ARKANSAS BUSINESS RADIO X

Alan Kay, an educator and computer pioneer, once observed, "The best way to predict the future is to invent it" (TED, n.d.). Expecting to hit the bull's eye each time you invent something is setting yourself up for failure. The same can be said about AI-powered tools. A case in point is Microsoft's Tay project. Tay was a chatbot built to converse with social media users and learn from them. Microsoft canned the project a day after Tay made offensive, racist, and sexist remarks (Rai, 2023).

As with Tay, your ChatGPT usage may deliver a different result. Some outcomes will be easy to spot, while others may prove difficult. One action that can ensure that you identify the impact of ChatGPT on your business's performance is measurement. This chapter is all about the importance of measuring the effectiveness of ChatGPT on your business for continuous improvement purposes.

ASSESSING THE IMPACT OF CHATGPT ON YOUR BUSINESS

There are numerous reasons for ongoing monitoring of the performance of your ChatGPT efforts, including the following:

- **You'll identify business issues in time.** It's commonly said that a trend is your friend in the financial markets. The same thinking works when in business. Routinely monitoring your ChatGPT's metrics reveals whether your performance is improving, stagnant, or declining. If the performance declines, you can dig deeper into the data to spot factors responsible for the poor performance. For instance, if your ChatGPT emails are generating lower open rates than usual, it's a sign that you need to refine them. You can fix them by crafting and testing compelling headlines and the preview text your readers see before opening the emails. Identifying performance issues before they become too big and expensive to solve keeps you in control of your business.

- **You'll improve your business's efficiencies.** In the early stages of your ChatGPT implementation, you won't know what performance standards you achieve. Over time, by measuring and refining your ChatGPT's performance, you'll create standards that improve business efficiencies. For example, you may discover the ideal prompts for generating more upsell sales and make them part of your operating standard.

- **You'll save money.** As mentioned above, routine monitoring helps you catch business issues quickly and improves efficiencies. Detecting business issues early minimizes the cost of fixing them when they have become massive. Improved business efficiencies reduce waste and decrease operational and production costs, leading to increased profits. Your revenues may also increase when you improve customer support efficiencies. The reason is that your customers will be more satisfied and stay longer with your business. This will increase customer lifetime value—how much each customer is worth.

- **You'll allocate resources better.** While ChatGPT can save resources like time and effort, improvement opportunities will always exist. As you routinely monitor ChatGPT's performance, you'll identify areas where you could allocate more time, money, or effort. This is particularly important when you're integrating ChatGPT into your business systems. For instance, if your data tells you that you have optimized your ChatGPT's lead generation efforts, you can shift resources to another area, such as customer service.

- **You can identify business scaling opportunities.** Proper ChatGPT usage should enable you to scale your business more quickly. You can't successfully scale unless you have first stabilized your business. You need to monitor your ChatGPT's performance to avoid scaling at the wrong time. The trends will tell you when you have reached that stability. Remember to scale only when you have developed systems for all your major business functions, such as marketing, information technology, sales, production, finance, and logistics.

The example metrics we have provided for the reasons mentioned earlier aren't exclusive. You can monitor many more metrics, depending on your objectives for introducing ChatGPT. We covered some of these metrics in Chapter 5, and others you may consider monitoring include revenue, gross profit, operating profit, net profit, and the customer retention rate.

How to Evaluate ChatGPT Usage in Your Business

Introducing a new technology such as ChatGPT into your business shouldn't be a haphazard process. Making those mistakes can shift your focus from what matters to spending time on unprofitable business activities. It's absolutely necessary to give time and thought to your implementation of ChatGPT. This will simplify the evaluation of this tool's usage in your business. The following steps will come in handy when thinking about ChatGPT implementation:

- **Step 1—set goals or milestones.** Whether you're using ChatGPT for lead generation and sales, customer service, or marketing, it's worth knowing how well it's performing. This is where identifying metrics to measure and ongoing monitoring come in. The starting point is to identify key performance indicators (KPIs) or metrics that measure the performance of ChatGPT in the areas you're using. Some metrics you may use include leads to customer conversion rate, customer inquiry response time, and customer acquisition cost. For each metric, determine the minimum level of ChatGPT performance you desire. For example, you can set a goal or milestone of reducing the number of customer complaints by 25% in the next six months.

- **Step 2—create a business monitoring dashboard.** A dashboard provides a centralized place to spot how your business is performing visually. It doesn't have to be an elaborate tool; a simple spreadsheet can be adequate. If you have the funds, you can purchase business dashboard software. When you set up your dashboard, include all the ChatGPT-related metrics so that you can identify relationships between them on one screen.

- **Step 3—measure ChatGPT's performance.** Once you've identified the metrics to measure and set up a dashboard, it's time to collect business data. Gather a variety of data that measures the metrics you've identified above. Your data can be both quantitative and qualitative.

- **Step 4—analyze your results.** In the beginning, give yourself enough time to collect your data. Some metrics, such as customer satisfaction, may take a while to collect enough data about them. For many of your metrics, two weeks to one month will be enough to gauge the performance of ChatGPT in your business. Once you have gathered enough data, analyze the trends you observe on your dashboard. The key here is to establish if you're hitting your goals, and if not, figure out what may not be working properly. Then, dig for reasons for poor performance and fix them. If there are no issues, repeat steps 1 through 4 with new goals or milestones.

Continuous improvement is the mark of great businesses. When your ChatGPT delivers as per your expectations, don't fold your arms satisfactorily. Instead, set new goals or milestones to grow your business. You don't need to set earth-shattering goals; they just have to be bigger than the previous ones so that you can hit higher revenue and profit levels.

STRATEGIES FOR IMPROVING CHATGPT PERFORMANCE

It can be frustrating when you've integrated ChatGPT into your business and yet not seen the benefits you expected. As you monitor your business's performance, you may notice that metrics such as customer satisfaction rates, social media engagement rates, and website bounce rates aren't improving. You'll probably feel like you wasted time, money, and effort to add ChatGPT to your business. Understand that business doesn't always go as we plan, especially when we introduce new initiatives; the success of your ChatGPT integration depends on how well you respond when the results aren't as you desired favor. The good news is that you can do something to turn around or improve the situation. All it takes is knowing what levers to touch and in what manner. This section will guide you on how to solve ChatGPT issues that prevent you from hitting the targets you have set.

Your strategies for improving ChatGPT's performance will vary depending on how you use it. If you're directly leveraging ChatGPT by using prompts, you'll apply different strategies from when you have built your own ChatGPT models.

How to Improve ChatGPT's Performance By Using Prompts

Suppose you primarily use ChatGPT for inspiration and creating content for business activities like lead generation, customer service, and marketing. In that case, prompts can make or break your efforts. They're often the reason metrics such as leads-to-sales conversion rates, social media engagement rates, customer satisfaction rates, and email open rates may be lower than you expected when you started using ChatGPT.

Refining your prompts can be the most potent masterstroke you can execute. Here are some of the strategies you can use to improve your prompts, irrespective of their purpose:

- **Start your prompts with verbs.** A verb specifies what you exactly want ChatGPT to do. For example, a prompt starting with the word "Compile" will differ from another beginning with the phrase "Can you." When your prompt isn't specific, the response you'll get will be generic and unhelpful.

- **Add context to your prompts.** When you provide ChatGPT with context, you force it to look for a specific response. If you want to improve customer satisfaction, tell ChatGPT why you wish to do so. For instance, you could tell the program that you've been using ChatGPT to provide customer support, but your customers are unhappy. Then, continue to say that you now want to improve customer satisfaction levels in your type of business. Also, state the kind of product you sell and who is your ideal target audience. The more background information you provide, the better the responses ChatGPT delivers.

- **Use a role-play prompt.** This prompt positions ChatGPT as an expert in a topic or business role where you could seek assistance. We've used these kinds of prompts in earlier chapters. If your lead generation prompts don't perform well, you could craft ChatGPT as a lead generation expert in your field. Mention its experience in lead generation and what accomplishments it has had in this role. Instruct it to use its expertise to help you improve your lead generation efforts.

- **Reference website pages or blog posts for improved style and tone.** If you know website pages or blog posts are written in a manner you'd like to mimic, reference them in your prompts. If you know which websites your target audience visits often, use them as references. Be careful to make sure that ChatGPT doesn't plagiarize the content on those websites.

- **Specify the length of the response you want.** ChatGPT has no way of knowing how long the answer you want it to be. Tell it precisely the number of words you need.

Prompting ChatGPT isn't a science but a combination of science and art. The perfect prompt will include all the elements discussed above. To generate the most effective prompt for your situation, refining the ones you're already using is your best bet. Through iteration, you'll have responses that help you improve ChatGPT's performance.

While it's crucial to get your ChatGPT prompting spot-on, it's essential to understand your business before using ChatGPT. Every response you require from ChatGPT should be based on your business. It's necessary to understand your industry, customers, and competitors for improved prompt generation.

What to Do If You Don't Attract Visitors to Your Website

Imagine that you've worked days and hours to craft powerful content, such as blog posts and product descriptions. When you check the number of visitors to your website, bounce rate, or sales, you don't seem to be doing well. You'll probably wonder how this could be.

ChatGPT can help you rank higher on search engines and receive more visitors to your website. This can increase leads and sales, provided your website copy is compelling and persuasive. When this isn't happening, the causal factors may be beyond the quality of your ChatGPT prompts. If you aren't driving an increased number of visitors to your website, your blog posts or product descriptions probably aren't SEO-optimized.

To SEO-optimize your blog posts, here's what to do:

- **Use ChatGPT to generate keyword ideas.** Your prompts should include your industry, the kind of product or service you sell, and your target audience. Remember to specify the number of keywords you want.
- **Check the search volumes** of each keyword with tools like Ahrefs Keyword Explorer, Semrush Keyword Magic Tool, or Google Keyword Planner.
- **Evaluate the difficulty of ranking for each of the keywords.** Prioritize the keywords in terms of this difficulty.
- **Select keywords with lower difficulty of ranking and good search volumes.** Note that a good search volume varies by industry, type of

business, season, and digital marketing goals. When you start, target search volumes between 100 and 1,000 monthly searches.

- For each blog post idea, **use ChatGPT to create an outline.**
- **Instruct ChatGPT to write each blog post based on the outline.** For each blog post, instruct ChatGPT on what keyword to use, how often to include the keyword, the word count of your blog, and tone and style. Also, tell it to add the keyword in all the headings, introductions, and meta descriptions, and end the blog with a call to action (CTA).
- **Refine your blog posts to sound like a human wrote them, and post to your website.** Remember to include links to high-authority websites.
- **Promote each blog post as soon as you publish it.** This is crucial to quickly get eyeballs on your content so that search engines may consider it significant. Many small business owners miss this. If you have a list of customers or an email list, send them the link to your blog post.

You can also optimize your product descriptions for search engines. The good news is that your website visitors attracted by product descriptions are people looking to buy. It's worth SEO-optimizing your product descriptions for customer attraction and sales generation. A good product description includes the product type and its features and benefits, uses compelling language, and targets your ideal customer's pain points or desires. A prompt like this is a good starting point to craft persuasive product descriptions:

"Craft a product description for [product name] that [benefits] promote [desired outcome] for [target customer] who [pain points or desires]."

STAYING AHEAD WITH UPCOMING AI AND CHATGPT TRENDS

The AI landscape keeps evolving, as you probably noted in its short history, as given in Chapter 1. The latest ChatGPT model we're enjoying using is also the result of constant iteration. This isn't going to stop soon, considering that numerous companies are developing new AI tools. Some of what you could expect to see in the future include the following:

- **Ethics and regulation:** We've stated earlier that AI and ChatGPT can infringe on people's rights and generate inaccurate facts. These issues and related ones will become concerns of the past as the AI sector enhances transparency and safety and introduces better practices. New York City has passed a law that requires employers to inform job applicants if they've used AI tools for recruitment purposes. In the EU, we can expect the new AI Act to be in force to regulate the use and development of AI tools.

- **AI-driven cybersecurity systems:** AI and ChatGPT use vast amounts of data that hackers can steal. To prevent this from happening, companies will develop more AI-driven cybersecurity systems to eliminate this threat. AI-driven cybersecurity systems respond faster to thwart any digital threat due to a data breach. The challenge is that attackers could also use similar technology to carry out their cyberattacks. Employing AI-driven cybersecurity systems will likely turn out to be a necessity.

- **Improvements in AI decision-making and problem-solving:** AI algorithms will become more sophisticated, enhancing the learning capabilities of AI systems. This will have significant implications in many industries, such as healthcare and automotive. In healthcare, the upgraded AI capabilities for decision-making and problem-solving may boost the diagnosing of diseases. Faster diagnosis means proper treatment can be administered in time, reducing the number of dying patients. In the automotive industry, AI has already been used successfully in developing autonomous vehicles. With more advanced AI, the journey to fully autonomous vehicles should be close to an end.

That's just a tiny sample of possible future AI developments that will affect how you do business and live your life. As an entrepreneur, you want to keep up with these developments to adjust your business. Some of the ways of staying updated with AI developments include these:

- **Check news on social media.** X (formerly Twitter) is arguably one of the platforms that technology companies use to share news. Having an X account and following key technology companies and news outlets will help you stay abreast with AI news.
- **Visit arXiV.org.** This source is great for finding the latest research papers about AI. It's a good idea to use this resource when looking for specific AI information because the number of papers about this field is vast.
- **Attend AI events and webinars.** Not only will AI events and webinars update you about the development in the industry, but you'll also access the best AI practices and applications. Check platforms like PyData, NeurIPS, Kaggle, and CVPR for the latest AI events and webinars.
- **Subscribe to relevant newsletters, online magazines, and YouTube channels that focus their content on AI.**
- **Create AI Google alerts.** When Google finds AI news on the internet, it'll drop you an email about it.

Monitoring the latest AI news will keep you in the know about what's happening in the industry. Staying abreast of these developments will enable you to adjust your AI strategies and implementation, keeping you ahead of your competitors.

Remember that you still need to evaluate the impact of ChatGPT on your business to ensure optimal results. Your dashboard will quickly show you which metrics you need to improve. In many cases, your improvements will require adjusting your ChatGPT prompts.

The strategies and knowledge in this book will help you continue to adapt and grow in the ever-evolving landscape of AI and ChatGPT. Keep in mind that the journey with ChatGPT and AI is a marathon, not a sprint, and this book has given you all the tools you need for the long haul.

Hello, fantastic readers!

As we near the end of our time together, I hope you gained ideas and perspective on ChatGPT, business, and the impacts AI will have in our society.

We would love to hear your feedback if you were compelled during this book. The need for your review is simple – it's about helping others, just as you were helped when you discovered the invaluable knowledge within these pages. Your insights guide fellow entrepreneurs, helping them navigate the intricate world of ChatGPT and AI.

So, here's the ask: Please take a few minutes to leave an honest review. It's your chance

to influence someone's entrepreneurial journey, offering insights, wisdom, and encouragement.

Here's how you can do it:

1. Visit the book's Amazon page by clicking the link or scanning the code below.
2. Scroll down to the 'Customer Reviews' section.
3. Click 'Write a customer review.'

https://www.amazon.com/review/create-review/?ie=
UTF8&channel=glance-detail&asin=B0CML6QC6F

Your review isn't just a few words; it's a gift to someone else. It's goodwill, support, and empowerment. By sharing your experience and insights, you're creating a ripple effect that can make the entrepreneurial path smoother for countless others.

Your support means the world to us, and we're excited to see the positive impact your review will have on others. Thank you for being part of the small business community, and here's to helping entrepreneurs everywhere thrive by Doing Business Right!

CONCLUSION

ChatGPT is not just making waves in the entrepreneurship community, but it's revolutionizing how business is conducted. Small businesses that don't adjust to the times will be left behind. It's crucial to understand the role of AI and ChatGPT and to protect yourself and your users when using these tools. This is precisely what this book intended to achieve in addition to helping you maximize your efficiencies to optimize your revenues and profits.

AI has existed for a couple of decades. It has now developed enough to become an ally to business owners and employees in carrying out tasks such as inventory management, customer service, accounting and finance, and navigating vehicles. Before you consider adding AI to your business, conducting a cost-benefit analysis is crucial to ensure it is worth doing so.

When a new technology shows up, people tend to doubt if it can do what the creators promise. The same thing is happening with AI and ChatGPT, which makes some small businesses reluctant to adopt it. Others are skeptical that ChatGPT can work for their businesses. For instance, they think ChatGPT is only for giant corporations. They forget that business functions are the same for all businesses, meaning you can use ChatGPT even if you're a one-person business.

The four areas we covered where ChatGPT can play a significant role are customer service, content creation, lead generation and sales, and data analysis. In each of these business functions, ChatGPT saves you time, improving efficiencies. For instance, by integrating ChatGPT with your customer support system, you can automate customer service. Your ChatGPT integration can also be helpful in the other three business areas.

For each of these business functions, you can use ChatGPT as it is. Unfortunately, you can't automate those processes since you'll need to create prompts. Your prompts can help you create customer surveys, resolve customer issues, craft engaging blog posts, compose social media posts, analyze all kinds of business data, and generate leads and sales. For each of your prompts to be effective, you need to instruct ChatGPT what roles it should play, your objective, and your guidance to be specific and concise. In case you want content generated, be sure to mention the kind of style and tone you want.

Remember to check the accuracy of facts and statistics that ChatGPT provides.

Proper ChatGPT integration into your business systems is imperative to realize the optimal impact of this tool. It involves identifying business systems to integrate with ChatGPT, setting integration goals, and choosing your integration method. If you opt to create a custom ChatGPT integration, you'll need to develop your tool for each of your systems.

Once you've created a prototype, test and refine it. When it's good, train your employees on it and then deploy it. Measure its performance and refine it when you encounter issues. For instance, your users might have difficulty interacting with your tool. Reasons for this include OpenAI server connectivity issues. Check the status of OpenAI on its website. Most importantly, when you face ChatGPT troubles, inform your users as soon as possible, as that is customer support at its best.

There are legal and ethical implications when you use AI and ChatGPT. It's crucial to comply with laws such as copyright and data privacy regulations. This is because ChatGPT was trained on a considerable amount of online information that may include copyrighted content. If you want ChatGPT to help you maximize revenues and opti-mize your efficiencies, it's crucial to comply with all online laws. Most often, the legal implications of using ChatGPT tend to be similar to mainstream ethical considerations. For instance, copyright infringement is both a legal and ethical concern. The primary ethical issue to keep in mind is plagiarism. Check the ChatGPT-produced content against plagiarism detectors to ensure you maintain the reputation of your brand.

Compliance with online laws and regulations isn't enough to continually enjoy the benefits of ChatGPT. Since the technology is new, you can expect plenty of changes as time progresses. For instance, the technology is likely to improve and become better, laws and regulations might change, and AI might help develop fully autonomous vehicles. You'll need to stay abreast of developments like this for your business to remain competitive. Use sources such as social media, newsletters, magazines, and Google alerts to keep yourself informed about AI and ChatGPT.

Proper use of AI and ChatGPT can take your business to another level. For instance, Beacon Street Services, a subsidiary of MarketWise, wanted to improve its sales and marketing. It used its AI platform to analyze massive amounts of data. It identified criteria that buyers used to make purchase decisions. Not only did Beacon Street Services increase sales by 10%, but it has also achieved 30 to 35 ROI (Violino, 2021). You can achieve similar results, or better, by deploying AI and ChatGPT into your business.

You now have the knowledge, and it's time to take action. Don't wait for the future to shape your business; use

ChatGPT to shape the direction of your business starting today!

We hope you have enjoyed reading this book. If you've identified at least one way you can use ChatGPT in your business or life when reading this book, we'd appreciate it if you could leave a review. Your feedback will help share the word with other entrepreneurs and improve future versions of this book!

BONUS MATERIAL

ChatGPT PROMPTS
<u>for Small Business Owners and Entrepreneurs</u>

Scan the QR Code or click the link to get a copy of ALL
the prompts
used in this book plus MORE!

https://docs.google.com/spreadsheets/d/
1ZjxoZnFVtYKzfXhdDMA5nQ-
Ifj6CtEsXfql7Uuvjcj0/copy

If you have any issues or questions, contact Dr. Bryan
Raya directly at
bryan@dbrbookkeeping.com

or visit his website
www.dbrbookkeeping.com

REFERENCES

Aaltonen, A. (2023, July 18). *Empowering content creation: Real-life success stories of generative AI speed, cost, and efficiency Improvements.* LinkedIn. https://www.linkedin.com/pulse/empowering-content-creation-real-life-success-stories-aaltonen/

Adrianne, P. (2023, September 27). *Success stories of organizations harnessing AI and business intelligence for transformative outcomes.* LinkedIn. https://www.linkedin.com/pulse/success-stories-organi zations-harnessing-ai-business-phillips/

Aguilhar, L. (n.d.). *How each social network counts video views.* Strike Social. https://strikesocial.com/blog/what-counts-as-a-view-on-social-media/

Arasa, D. (2023, May 5). *From ChatGPT to cha-ching: Inspiring chatbot success stories.* INQUIRER.net. https://technology.inquirer.net/123804/the-top-five-chatbot-success-stories

Barker, J. (2023, February 17). *Social advertising benchmarks for 2023.* Brafton. https://www.brafton.com/blog/social-media/social-adver tising-benchmarks/

Bernazzani, S. (2022, March 11). *The ultimate guide to customer retention.* Hubspot. https://blog.hubspot.com/service/customer-retention

Bilan, M. (2023, September 26). *Statistics of ChatGPT & generative AI in business: 2023 report.* Master of Code Global. https://masterofcode. com/blog/statistics-of-chatgpt-generative-ai-in-business-2023-report

BrainyQuote. (n.d.). *Peter Drucker quotes.* https://www.brainyquote. com/quotes/peter_drucker_131600

Burstein, D. (2023, July 19). *Mastering the art of the business pivot: Real-life examples and success stories about an AI chatbot, ChatGPT prompts, and a business model shift.* MarketingSherpa. https://www.marketing sherpa.com/article/case-study/business

Cornell, J. (2022, May 31). *How many questions should be asked in a survey?* ProProfs. https://www.proprofssurvey.com/blog/how-many-questions-asked-in-survey/

Frey, C. B., & Osborne, M. (2013). *The future of employment*. Oxford Martin School. https://www.oxfordmartin.ox.ac.uk/downloads/academic/future-of-employment.pdf

Gualtieri, M. (2016, January 22). *Hadoop is data's darling for a reason*. Forrester. https://www.forrester.com/blogs/hadoop-is-datas-darling-for-a-reason/

Hines, K. (2023, April 11). *ChatGPT and generative AI tools face legal woes worldwide*. Search Engine Journal. https://www.searchenginejournal.com/chatgpt-legal-woes/484323/#close

Hu, K. (2023, February 2). ChatGPT sets record for fastest-growing user base - analyst note. *Reuters*. https://www.reuters.com/technology/chatgpt-sets-record-fastest-growing-user-base-analyst-note-2023-02-01/

Kemp, S. (2023, April 27). *Digital 2023 april global statshot report*. Data-Reportal. https://datareportal.com/reports/digital-2023-april-global-statshot

Lanier, S. (2023, June 13). *Content marketing cost: Is it worth it? (+ Examples)*. HawkSEM. https://hawksem.com/blog/content-marketing-cost/

Main, K. (2022, December 7). *Small business statistics of 2023* (C. Bottorff, Ed.). Forbes. https://www.forbes.com/advisor/business/small-business-statistics/

Merriam-Webster. (n.d.). *Definition of skepticism*. https://www.merriam-webster.com/dictionary/skepticism

Mueller, A. (2022, April 8). *The cost of hiring a new employee*. Investopedia. https://www.investopedia.com/financial-edge/0711/the-cost-of-hiring-a-new-employee.aspx

Newberry, C., & McLachlan, S. (2023, September 23). *Social media for business: A practical guide*. Hootsuite. https://blog.hootsuite.com/social-media-for-business/

Nucleus_AI. (2023, April 3). *ChatGPT as CEO: Startup's €400,000 profit & rapid success with AI*. YourStory. https://yourstory.com/2023/04/chatgpt-ai-ceo-profitable-startup-aisthetic-apparel

OpenAI. (2023, June 23). *Privacy policy*. https://openai.com/policies/

privacy-policy

Podium. (2022, November 8). *8 benefits of social media marketing for small businesses*. https://www.podium.com/article/social-media-benefits-for-small-businesses/

Rai, S. (2023, April 9). *Failed AI projects that went terribly wrong: The dark side of artificial intelligence*. DATAQUEST. https://www.dqindia.com/failed-ai-projects-that-went-terribly-wrong-the-dark-side-of-artificial-intelligence/

Riddall, J. (2023, January 6). *30 content marketing statistics you should know*. Search Engine Journal. https://www.searchenginejournal.com/content-marketing-statistics/475206/#close

Rybakova, M. (2022, June 22). *HelloFresh creates customer service chatbot with Chatfuel*. Chatfuel. https://chatfuel.com/blog/hellofresh-reduces-support-wait-times-with-chatfuel-messenger-bot

Saleh, K. (2023, July 14). *The importance of lead nurturing*. Invesp. https://www.invespcro.com/blog/lead-nurturing/

Sidor, J. (2023, April 17). *5 advantages of customer service automation*. Zowie. https://getzowie.com/blog/advantages-customer-service-automation

Tableau. (n.d.). *What is the history of artificial intelligence (AI)?* https://www.tableau.com/data-insights/ai/history

Taheer, F. (2023, September 8). *Online Review Statistics You Need To Know in 2023 - TrustPulse*. TrustPulse. https://trustpulse.com/online-review-statistics/

TED. (n.d.). *TED speaker: Alan Gray*. https://www.ted.com/speakers/alan_kay

U.S. Bureau of Labor Statistics. (2023). *The employment situation - September 2023*. https://www.bls.gov/news.release/pdf/empsit.pdf

Violino, B. (2021, April 26). *3 enterprise AI success stories*. InfoWorld. https://www.infoworld.com/article/3615449/3-enterprise-ai-success-stories.html

WebFX. (n.d.). *Website copywriter pricing: How much does copywriting cost?* https://www.webfx.com/content-marketing/pricing/website-copywriting/

Weston, B. (2022, May 10). *Infographic: Are you taking advantage of marketing data?* Score. https://www.score.org/resource/blog-post/

infographic-are-you-taking-advantage-marketing-data

Zendesk. (n.d.). *CX trends 2022*. https://cdn2.assets-servd.host/paltry-coyote/production/exports/2194a329d6f053118e42d885fe38fae7/zendesk-cx-trends-2022-report.pdf

Zhou, L. (2023, July 28). https://www.luisazhou.com/blog/businesses-that-fail/

ABOUT THE AUTHOR AND PUBLISHER

DBR Publishing was founded by Dr. Bryan Raya in 2023. Dr. Raya is an entrepreneur, U.S. Army Veteran, musician, educator, and host of the Doing Business Right Podcast. After studying project management, bookkeeping, and marketing, Dr. Raya started DBR Bookkeeping in 2022 to help entrepreneurs and small businesses. Dr. Raya strongly advocates for entrepreneurship, personal empowerment, the arts, and effective team collaboration. He currently resides in Fayetteville, Arkansas, where he is active in the small business community and continues to help, inspire, and share the stories and perspectives of others with the community.

DBR Publishing is committed to providing authoritative and practical resources for small businesses and entrepreneurs. We are dedicated to helping small business owners navigate the complex world of business and finance, empowering them to make informed decisions that drive growth and success.

We believe in a comprehensive yet accessible approach to entrepreneurship and small business practices. Our publications are designed to demystify financial and business concepts, breaking them into practical, easy-to-understand terms. We prioritize offering streamlined strategies and proven techniques that entrepreneurs can implement without unnecessary complexity or jargon.

At DBR Publishing, we advocate for sound financial practices rooted in ethics and integrity. We understand the importance of Doing Business Right, and our books reflect this commitment by providing guidance on ethical decision-making and responsible business practices. By empowering small business owners with the knowledge and tools to make informed financial choices, we contribute to a stronger, more resilient small business ecosystem.

You can connect with Dr. Bryan Raya here:

https://www.dbrbookkeeping.com

https://www.linkedin.com/company/dbr-bookkeeping

https://www.facebook.com/DBRBookkeeping

OTHER BOOKS BY DBR PUBLISHING
AND DR. BRYAN RAYA

The Essential Small Business Guide to Financial Management

Streamlined Strategies for Maximized Profits, Compliance, and Long-Term Success

for Money-Stressed Entrepreneurs

By DBR Publishing

https://www.amazon.com/Essential-Small-Business-Financial-Management/dp/B0CJDDG79S/ref=tmm_pap_swatch_0?_encoding=UTF8&qid=1698616677&sr=1-1

(**Read Now**)

Quick Advice to Promote Your Business from Ground Zero

Simple Tips to Overcome Early Marketing Challenges

for Entrepreneurs on a Tight Budget

By Dr. Bryan Raya

https://www.amazon.com/Quick-Advice-Promote-Business-Ground/dp/B0CDK3ZPZQ/ref=tmm_pap_swatch_0?_encoding=UTF8&qid=1698616327&sr=1-1

Read Now

Made in the USA
Columbia, SC
05 January 2025

51272973R00117